50
SUCCESSFUL
HARVARD
APPLICATION
ESSAYS
FIFTH EDITION

Also by the Staff of The Harvard Crimson

50
SUCCESSFUL
HARVARD
APPLICATION
ESSAYS

FIFTH EDITION

With Analysis by the Staff of *The Harvard Crimson*

ST. MARTIN'S GRIFFIN NEW YORK

www.stmartins.com

The Library of Congress Cataloging-in-Publication Data is available upon request.

ISBN 978-1-250-12755-6 (trade paperback)
ISBN 978-1-250-12756-3 (e-book)

Our books may be purchased in bulk for promotional, educational, or business use. Please contact your local bookseller or the Macmillan Corporate and Premium Sales Department at 1-800-221-7945, extension 5442, or by e-mail at MacmillanSpecialMarkets@macmillan .com.

First Edition: May 2017

10 9 8 7 6 5 4 3

CONTENTS

Contents

III. Identity

IV. Overcoming Obstacles

V. Experiences Abroad

Contents

VI. Cultural Identity

ACKNOWLEDGMENTS

I would first like to thank our fantastic editor, Laura Apperson, for helping us write the fifth edition of this book—we could not have done it without her guidance and expert advice. I am also grateful for the dozens of Harvard undergraduates who submitted their essays to this book in order to help other students get into the college of their dreams. I also want to thank the *Crimson* staff writers who stepped up to write reviews of the terrific essays collected in this book. Finally, I'd like to thank the members of the *Crimson* staff who made this book a success: Hannah Shen, Harriet Tieh, Leia Wedlund, Meg Bernhard, Ivan Levingston, Matt Clarida, and Lauren Volpert.

—MARIEL A. KLEIN

President, the 143rd Guard of *The Harvard Crimson*

PREFACE

"I first performed brain surgery before I learned how to drive."

These words were memorable enough to help move a Harvard applicant from the ranks of the 39,000 who applied to the list of the 2,000 who were admitted.

Whether you're applying to Harvard or another school, you need an essay that sets you apart from thousands of others. Here's the good news: by picking up this helpful book, you're on the right track, and as long as you don't wait until the night before the deadline (or make the mistake of applying to Yale), things are looking up!

In the essay portion of your application, you're tasked with thoughtfully revealing who you are beyond your grades, test scores, and activities. The essay is a chance for you to breathe life into a one-dimensional file and offer colleges a more personal and colorful picture. There's no foolproof formula for writing a successful college essay. But if you read this book and follow our advice, you will start to view the essay as an opportunity, not an obstacle.

Standout essays—like those in this book—make the reader feel connected to the writer. The spark that ignites that connection could be a moment of surprise, a pang of sadness, a feeling of warmth and happiness, genuine laughter, disbelief, or intrigue.

We're featuring a wide variety of essays in this edition of this book. A high school student body president opens up about being homeless for five years. A young woman with East Indian heritage describes what it's like to live in a tumbleweed town in Texas. A student who was the editor in chief of his high school newspaper waxes poetic about his passion for jazz.

Many of these essays are not necessarily unique in the choice of

Preface

topics (service experience and overcoming failure are common themes), but they're evocative by virtue of introspection, the creativity of prose, an authentic expression of passion, and the ability to produce real emotion in their readers.

While this book features excellent essays from students who were admitted to Harvard, it's intended to be useful for all students applying to college. We hope you will use the words on these pages as a source of inspiration. New in the fifth edition are profile details about each writer that will help you understand the context behind their submissions—and how your own experiences might inform a strong essay.

So, as you place your fingers on your keyboard or take pen to paper, remember your essay should be as unique as you are; there's no right or wrong topic. What do you go to bed thinking about? What gets your heart racing with excitement in the morning? That's where you start.

Best of luck!

—Mariel A. Klein
President, the 143rd Guard of *The Harvard Crimson*

I. PASSION

In the preface, we told you to infuse your essay with passion. But it's not enough to write a laundry list of the things you've done that demonstrate your commitment to your passion. An essay about passion should follow the tried and true writing adage: Show, don't tell. The key to success in these essays is identifying a specific anecdote that demonstrates your unbridled passion for whatever you do.

In the following essays, you will read about how a student's love for the Beatles became an exploration of new musical experiences, and how another student's interest in animal languages allowed her to reflect on human communication.

Pay close attention to the depth of description all of the students use in discussing their passions. Their passions themselves are not unique—music, medicine, and art are common interests for many people—but the way these writers talk about their passions conveys a sense of excitement. The applicants demonstrate a strong commitment to a particular subject or field, but to make their essays stand out, they use descriptive language and narratives that allow the reader to feel their enthusiasm for what they love.

Michael Bervell

Hometown: Mukilteo, Washington, USA
High School: Public school, 550 students in graduating class
Ethnicity: Black, African American
Gender: Male
GPA: 3.9 out of 4.0
SAT: Reading 800, Math 800, Writing 800
ACT: 35
SAT Subject Tests Taken: Mathematics Level 1, Mathematics Level 2, Physics, World History
Extracurriculars: Student body president; newspaper editor in chief; varsity debate captain; Hugs for Ghana (nonprofit) cofounder and executive director; GMAZ Jazz Quartet cofounder, drummer, and manager
Awards: International Build-a-Bear Workshop Huggable Heroes Award, National Bank of America Student Leader Delegate, Evergreen Boys State Delegate and Governor, National Radio Disney Hero for Change Award, National Achievement Scholar, National Coca-Cola Scholar
Major: Philosophy and Computer Science

ESSAY

"A-one," I adjust my earphones.

"A-two," I wipe the sweat off my sticks.

"A-one-two-three-four!" The sharp rhythm of Mr. Dizzy Gillespie's iconic bebop tune "Salt Peanuts" rattles through my head like saline seeds as I silently count myself off. Then—without a hitch—Gillespie, his quintet, and I are off.

My left foot taps the AP biology textbook, my sticks bounce along the metal frame of my bed, and my soul dances to the beat I am creating. This makeshift drum set is a liberating entrance into an abstract world where I am free to express myself. As I sit on the edge of my bed imitating the monophonic flow of drummer Max Roach, I close my eyes and envision myself performing onstage with world-renowned Gillespie. We stand before thousands of people, steeped in the spotlight's brilliant glare, and as we play my arms become a flurry of motion when, suddenly, *crack*!

I snap back into reality and my eyes shoot open only to realize that the moment of pure ecstasy had been interrupted—another broken drumstick!

Smiling, I pick up the pieces and walk toward a worn, old, black Ikea desk in the corner of my room. Since 5th grade, my DrumDrawer has been the keeper of every pair of new and broken drumsticks I have ever owned.

I pull open the big bottom drawer and stand admiring the sacred splinters for a brief moment before finally dropping in this latest offering. The sticks in my small pine sepulcher illustrate the quintessential facets of who I am—a musician, leader, and philanthropist. While most people typically collect rocks or baseball cards, I collect musical phrases from my life and store them in this drawer.

As I reach to the bottom, my fingers wrap around two white Vic Firth sticks. Rubbing my fingers along the bumps on the wood, I grin. This exclusive pair shared my accomplishments of playing jazz under the Eiffel Tower in Paris, drumming in award-winning spring musicals, and being inducted into the National Tri-M Music Honor Society. Moreover, these sticks not only inspired me to persevere as I cofounded, managed, and drummed in the GMAZ Jazz Quartet, but they also instilled confidence in me when I needed it most.

After I decided to run for Student Body President of my 2,200-student high school in what turned out to be a competitive election against two of my closest friends, these tattered drumsticks soothed and comforted me. Despite turbulent weeks of campaigning and preparing a daunting school-wide campaign speech, I always looked forward to returning to my bedroom and playing my favorite jazz melodies. The ups and downs of musical arrangements never failed to strike a chord.

Reminiscing, I twirl the white drumsticks between my fingers and realize that they also profoundly influenced my view of service. Once a month, these wooden wonders and I would trek from my desk to the local retirement home where we performed with other musicians in monthly "Play-It-Forward" retirement home concerts. On these Friday nights, my sticks danced on the drums, our music floated throughout the concert hall, elderly faces glowed, and I was free to let out my creative exuberance. In organizing dozens of these events, I have shared with both peers and audience members my own musical definition of altruism.

I return my Vic Firth sticks to the drawer and contentedly appreciate the collection of memories. While the wooden contents physically have no other value than, perhaps, kindling a small fire, I cannot bear to part with them. Someday the sticks will go, I realize, but the music will not.

Fresh pair of sticks in hand, I slowly shut the DrumDrawer, return to my bed, and count myself off, eyes closed, to John Coltrane's jazz rendition of "My Favorite Things" by Richard Rodgers and Oscar Hammerstein.

"A-one, a-two, a-one-two-three-four!"

REVIEW

Right from the introduction, readers are thrown into the vibrant and colorful world that Michael's essay creates. Passion for a musical instrument is a topic that is doubtlessly written about by many applicants, but Michael differentiates himself by using his passion for drumming to demonstrate his stylistic flair, cleverly finding ways to discuss his other, non-musical accomplishments and pursuits.

Michael clearly aims to communicate that he is a "musician, leader, and philanthropist" throughout his essay—a goal he successfully accomplishes. His musical talent and passion come alive through the vivid imagery and onomatopoeia that he uses. To demonstrate leadership, he shows how he dealt with a difficult situation maturely. Finally, his dedication to volunteer work is seamlessly worked into the essay when he recalls playing concerts at a retirement home.

Michael roots the essay in the physical space of his bedroom, but chooses a place that allows him to be creative and cover a lot of aspects of himself that might not be accessible in other parts of his application. The full-circle ending is a nice touch to further root the essay in the prompt. Michael does a wonderful job of demonstrating that you don't need a particularly unique topic to create a memorable essay.

—Mia Karr

JANG LEE

Hometown: Flower Mound, Texas, USA
High School: Public school, 816 students in graduating class
Ethnicity: Asian
Gender: Male
GPA: 4.0 out of 4.0
SAT: Reading 800, Math 740, Writing 790
ACT: n/a
SAT Subject Tests Taken: Mathematics Level 2, Chemistry
Extracurriculars: President of art club / National Art Honor Society, vice president of Science National Honor Society, founding member and vice president of creative engagement and design for 501(c)3 nonprofit Raise4aCause, volunteer at church summer school
Awards: PSAT semifinalist, Welch Summer Scholar, 1 Scholastic Silver Key and 2 Gold Keys, artwork exhibited at the Texas Legislative Budget Board and part of the Texas Art Education Association traveling exhibition, Gold Seal at UIL Texas art competition (highest possible award given to .6% of artworks out of over twenty thousand submissions)
Major: Visual and Environmental Studies

ESSAY

Like it does on most nights, the smell of toxic fumes drifts through my room.

Occasionally washing my paintbrushes in turpentine oil thinner,

7

I am uncomfortably aware that these vapors can cause brain damage, lung cancer, and chronic respiratory problems. My lifelong passion is killing me—*literally*. Yet, this smell is strangely comforting. It blankets me with a sense of security I find nowhere else.

An artist at the core, my paint-smeared heart pumps pigments of red through veins and arteries—the love for painting permeates every part of my body and has transformed me. By constantly observing subtle details of objects, breathtaking spectrums of color, and the interactions of lights and darks, my perception of the world has shifted.

I walk down the school hallway during passing period. Carried by a stream of teenage bodies, I notice ceiling lights scattering among clothes and locks of glossy hair. Looking down, shadows crisscross and overlap on the laminated floor to create a kaleidoscope of dancing silhouettes. Faces draw my attention—delicate hues of rosy pink on tips of ears and softly chiseled curves of bone. I observe my surroundings from an artist's perspective, fully immersed in a state of perpetual learning.

Ultimately, my goal as an artist is to give my art personal, profound depth that transcends aesthetic purpose or technical skill. Paintings do not have to be of flowers or landscapes; they can portray story, emotion, and experience. Consequently, my art is inspired by personal experiences and observations. I hope to convey a fresh perspective of my life through strokes of color. The ambition of creating depth in my art forces me to reflect on myself as I continually ask *why* I am painting *what* I am painting. And because of the rigorous reflection of my values and experiences, I am given a greater sense of self-identity. This overwhelming position as an artist is humbling, teaching me an appreciation for self-worth often neglected or trivialized in a fast-paced American lifestyle. I want to show others this same value through my art so they can slow down to recognize and appreciate the value of their own lives.

Wonderland Unknown, a painting based on my favorite childhood story, *Alice in Wonderland,* depicts a rabbit in a forest of overgrown mushrooms and twisted trees. The piece builds on the idea that children's innate creativity and capacity for imagination are stifled as they mature. Growing up, I began to feel estranged from the tale because it turned unrealistically ridiculous, a personal testimony to the slow deterioration of childhood wonder. Painting *Wonderland Unknown* was an epiphany—I realized that creativity is inherent: a universal thread within all of us that stitches humanity together. Most importantly, it is a trait that should be nurtured and valued instead of taken for granted.

Truly, art is a world of possibility and a world I would like to share.

It is a place where one is *encouraged* to break rules, be unapologetically audacious, and take pride in unorthodoxy. Ready to play creator of my universe, I rule with brush in one hand and palette in the other, painting because of a chance to explore this liberating world and discover myself through it. And in the end, art will always stay a constant in my life, forever my private sanctuary of creativity and personal expression. A place where I am infinite.

I feel relieved knowing that the smell of turpentine will always comfort me. It is a thin, oily smell of ironic undertones, vaguely nauseating and coffee-ground bitter. It is a smell that has given me life.

REVIEW

Jang's essay is filled with beautiful phrasing and flowery descriptions, which shows off his writing skills and creativity. One of the biggest strengths of the essay is how Jang pairs explanation of art's function in his life with an artistic analysis of the piece *Wonderland Unknown.*

Being able to write exceedingly well in a distinctive narrative form proves to be a strength for Jang. His essay weds two distinct types of writing—narrative and analytical—together, which is the very essence of what a good college essay should be. But, rather than present a single, overarching narrative, the writer takes the reader through separate vignettes: a crowded hallway, his work space at home, the scene depicted in the painting—all of which combine to provide a distinct and colorful look into the writer's relationship with art.

—Brandon J. Dixon

JOE KERWIN

Hometown: Medfield, Massachusetts, USA
High School: Private all-male school, 72 students in graduating class
Ethnicity: White
Gender: Male
GPA: 4.3 out of 4.0
SAT: Reading 800, Math 800, Writing 740
ACT: n/a
SAT Subject Tests Taken: Mathematics Level 2, Chemistry, Physics, Literature
Extracurriculars: Student body president; editor and contributor to the school literature and arts magazine, academic journal, and newspaper; guitarist and bassist in ensembles at school and at the New England Conservatory; guitar teacher at Pope John Paul II Academy
Awards: Williams College Book Award; Pursuit of Excellence awards in religion, music, and literature; Cum Laude Society; Saint Sebastian's Medal for Fine Arts', Cardinal Cushing Memorial Medal for Student Service
Major: History and Literature

ESSAY

Nothing could have prepared me for the first time I heard the jangle of John Lennon's Rickenbacker guitar that opens the theme song of the Beatles's film *A Hard Day's Night*. Thinking I might enjoy a movie that had played a part in her childhood, my mother exposed me to

11

the film, inadvertently sparking an obsession that may never fully subside.

I watched the film constantly until I had every tune and lyric of the soundtrack down. I could recite each line and mimic every one of the characters' gestures. A visitor entering my bedroom at this point would have been bombarded with Beatlemania, encountering posters, pins, T-shirts, and my personal favorite: a Beatles-themed lamp.

When my uncle learned of my fixation, he took me to buy my first guitar. As I began to explore other artists of the British invasion, I begged my parents to let me take lessons in order to emulate the sounds of my favorite artists. I took advantage of any free moment to sneak up to my bedroom and work my fingers into ready position to play the Who's "Pinball Wizard." I often stayed up until the early hours of the morning plucking the "My Generation" riff, crouched behind a wall of pillows I had constructed to prevent the twang of my guitar from traveling down the hallway and into my parents' bedroom.

Although the opening sound of A Hard Day's Night and the image of the Beatles fleeing a throng of bawling girls triggered many different thoughts, my immediate reaction was to know I needed to play in a band. I joined my school's pit band and began attending grueling two-hour practices in preparation for performances of musicals like Anything Goes and Guys and Dolls. Through the New England Conservatory, I attended classes and participated in small jazz combos. Though I collaborated on recordings of covers and original pieces with classmates as well as teachers, my most rewarding recording projects were the tracks I created with my brother. In these songs, we blended hip-hop style beats, rock instrumentation, and samples from vintage vinyl to create an aesthetic that we'd never heard before. Few feelings can compare to the fulfillment of playing back a piece of music I've created with a sound I believe to be completely my own.

Passion

Playing with others provides an escape from the obstacles that bog me down in other areas of my life, and when I lose myself in music, I am unfettered and uninhibited by my weaknesses.

Since I discovered my passion, I have accumulated a myriad of experiences that the pre-Beatles Joe could have never imagined. I am most proud of a service project I initiated that entailed weekly drives into Dorchester to share my passion with young students through guitar lessons. Many of my other musical adventures have transpired at events I attended. I spent hours in the pouring rain waiting for Wilco to perform at their eclectic indie festival in western Massachusetts. At one o'clock in the morning, I participated in a tribute to Don Cornelius featuring a "*Soul Train* line" at a poetry slam in the basement of the Lizard Lounge. In a welding shop tucked amid several warehouses, I attended a DIY punk show in Worcester and braved my first mosh pit.

This year marked the 50th anniversary of the release of A *Hard Day's Night*, and to honor the occasion, the film was reintroduced into theaters. Although much of the movie had faded from my memory, I made the trip north to Portland, Maine to see the film. As the lights in the State Theatre dimmed, I shivered in anticipation. This time, when I heard the familiar chord from that tinny twelve-string echo through the building, I knew I was in for something special.

REVIEW

The strength of Joe's writing in this essay lies in his anecdotal beginning and descriptive language throughout. His personality shines through as he reveals a comical and thoughtful character, for example, mentioning that his personal favorite piece of Beatles memorabilia is a lamp. The concluding paragraph also connects well with the introduction, creating a bookend effect.

Unfortunately, Joe's essay at times reads like a list of accomplishments. It would have been helpful if Joe had chosen one rewarding experience that stemmed from his discovery of the Beatles and expanded on it with an anecdote. For example, the service project he is "most proud of" is teaching guitar lessons to high school students in Dorchester. Yet, he offers little evidence to explain why.

—Beth Young

BRIANNA OPPONG-ANTWI

Hometown: Wrightsville, Pennsylvania, USA
High School: Public school, 170 students in graduating class
Ethnicity: Black, African American
Gender: Female
GPA: 4.52 out of 4.0
SAT: Reading 740, Math 620, Writing 690
ACT: 32
SAT Subject Tests Taken: Mathematics Level 1, Mathematics Level 2, Biology E/M, Chemistry, Literature, U.S. History
Extracurriculars: Founder and editor in chief of the newspaper the *Knightly Journal*, president of Eastern York High School Parliamentary Procedures Team, Model United Nations cocaptain and chairman of the World Health Organization, five-year Science Olympiad Division B and C medalist, freshman and sophomore class president
Awards: Valedictorian, AP Scholar with Honors, Pennsylvania School Board Association first-place essay contest and speech winner, *New York Times* Junior Essay Contest second-place winner, Minority Introduction to Engineering and Science first-place team in genomics research at the Broad Institute of MIT and Harvard
Major: Biomedical Engineering

ESSAY

I shouldn't be here right now. My life could have never been. There are 70 trillion genetic combinations to make human beings. Our chromosomes could have aligned to make the best human being: a person who has the strength of Lance Armstrong, the cunning of Albert Einstein, and the kindness of Mother Teresa all in one. But that didn't happen. Billions of chromosome combinations for a human being were possible, and I was born. I am not a superhuman being, but I do intend on making my life extraordinary.

I have every resource to make my life extraordinary. I know this because I am growing up in America, the land of opportunity. The land where anything is possible, as long as you work for it. My father came to America from Ghana with only a pair of pants, two shirts, and $100 in his pocket. Today, he is an engineer. He always expressed to me the value of education, and I remember the long car rides home from school when he would stress to me: "Brianna, hard work, hard work always pays off."

In my school, I am often the only black face in a classroom; but I do not let this bother me. In the classroom, regardless of race, gender, or interests, knowledge is the great equalizer. I know that the knowledge I gain is not only for myself, but for every child in Ghana. Some nights I stay up and think how my life would be the same as theirs if I hadn't been lucky enough to have parents that came to America. Since I am here, in America, I will make the most out of every opportunity. I will learn so that I can pass on the gift of learning. Every extra hour I study, every time I sacrifice going out with friends, every night I stay up late, I tell myself that it will all pay off for a greater cause.

Last summer I was given an extraordinary educational opportunity when I participated in the Minority Introduction to Engineering and Sciences (MITES). MITES is a six-week summer program at MIT that immersed me in an academic world I had never known. I was surrounded by some of the top students in the nation in an environment that pushed me to learn and see the world in ways I had never envisioned. That level of academia is something I love.

Passion

During MITES I had the opportunity to take a genomic elective at the Broad Institute of MIT and Harvard. On one of my last days there, I was standing in front of the Broad, and I looked up and realized it was here that I felt most alive. To know that I was about to enter a building that had so much potential to discover anything gave me a feeling of excitement and happiness I have never felt about anything else. It made me certain that I want to be a medical researcher.

In the lab, I was able to see for myself the capabilities of genomic research. The most fascinating and exciting part of all this was that it may soon be possible to tell exactly why someone is sick just by looking at their microbiome. This breakthrough would have enormously positive ramifications in Ghana and other parts of Africa.

My dream is to continue this research. The Broad is currently working on research in conjunction with Harvard that delves into areas that I envision great strides being made in. I want to contribute my knowledge and passion into these extraordinary strides.

Human genetics could have aligned to make a perfect human being, but they did not. They made me as I am now. I am aware that even though I may be flawed, I have been given this one precious life. At the end of my life I want to be able to honestly say that I used all the potential I was given; there is nothing left. Never before has there been so much technology, opportunity, and ability to make the absolute most out of a human life. And not only to improve one's own situation, but also the lives of others. I know that I would not have the opportunities granted to me if other people before me had not worked and innovated. I feel that it is my turn to innovate, to improve the lives of mankind for generations long after I am gone. To follow my passion and make my life absolutely extraordinary.

REVIEW

Brianna's essay does an excellent job of mixing together her own personal self-reflection on her values and mentality as well as anecdotes from her life that help to provide a clearer picture of her personality. While many applicants might choose to discuss one compelling idea through the lens of a single story, Brianna chooses to discuss her idea—namely, that she refuses to allow herself to stand in her own way—through multiple stories that all contribute to a larger narrative. Each paragraph stands alone as insight into Brianna's character as a motivated and determined person, but they weave together well. This sort of approach can sometimes be a bit risky: by telling too many different stories, an applicant runs the risk of not providing enough depth in each, but in general, this essay does a good job of remaining cohesive while still highlighting a variety of key stories that this applicant has to tell.

—Brian Yu

ELIZABETH SUN

Hometown: Troy, Michigan, USA
High School: Public school, 477 students in graduating class
Ethnicity: Asian
Gender: Female
GPA: 4.3 out of 5.0
SAT: Reading 780, Math 800, Writing 770
ACT: 35
SAT Subject Tests Taken: Chemistry, Literature, U.S. History, Chinese
Extracurriculars: Troy District FIRST Robotics Team (information vice president); clarinet (marching band squad leader, symphonic band, symphony orchestra); Project LEAD (elementary events chairperson and hemophilia party chairperson); poetry club (president and founder); art (NAHS member, assistant teacher at Art Longlong Studio)
Awards: USA Biology Olympiad semifinalist; National Merit finalist; State Fish Art Contest, first place; CLASS National Essay Gold Apple Award; Science Olympiad State Competition GeoLogic Mapping, first place
Major: Undecided

ESSAY

"Paint this vase before you leave today," my teacher directed as she placed foreign brushes and paints in my hands. I looked at her blankly. Where were the charts of colors and books of techniques? Why was her smile so decidedly encouraging? The sudden expectations made no sense.

She smiled. "Don't worry, just paint."

In a daze, I assembled my supplies the way the older students did. I was scared. I knew everything but nothing. And even in those first blissful moments of experimentation, it hurt to realize that my painting was all wrong. The gleam of light. The distorted reflection. A thousand details taunted me with their refusal to melt into the glass. The vase was lifeless at best.

As the draining hours of work wore on, I began wearing reckless holes in my mixing plate. It was my fourth hour here. Why had I not received even a single piece of guidance?

At the peak of my frustration, she finally reentered the studio, yawning with excruciating casualness. I felt myself snap.

"I barely know how to hold a brush," I muttered almost aggressively, "how could I possibly have the technique to paint this?"

She looked at me with a shocked innocence that only heightened the feeling of abandonment. "What do you mean you don't have the technique?"

It was as though she failed to realize I was a complete beginner.

And then suddenly she broke into a pitch of urgent obviousness: "What are you doing! Don't you see those details?? There's orange from the wall and light brown from the floor. There's even dark green from that paint box over there. You have to look at the whole picture," she stole a glance at my face of bewilderment, and, sighing, grabbed my paint-stained hand. "Listen, it's not in here," she implored, shaking my captive limb. "It's here." The intensity with which she looked into my eyes was overwhelming.

I returned the gaze emptily. Never had I been so confused . . .

But over the years I did begin to see. The shades of red and blue in gray concrete, the tints of Phthalo in summer skies, and winter's

Currelean. It was beautiful and illogical. Black was darker with green and red, and white was never white.

I began to study animals. The proportions and fan brush techniques were certainly difficult, but they were the simple part. It was the strategic tints of light and bold color that created life. I would spend hours discovering the exact blue that would make a fish seem on the verge of tears and hours more shaping a deer's ears to speak of serenity instead of danger.

In return for probing into previously ignored details, my canvas and paints opened the world. I began to appreciate the pink kiss of ever-evolving sunsets and the even suppression of melancholy. When my father came home from a business trip, it was no longer a matter of simple happiness, but of fatigue and gladness' underlying shades. The personalities who had once seemed so annoyingly arrogant now turned soft with their complexities of doubt and inspiration. Each mundane scene is as deep and varied as the paint needed to capture it.

One day, I will learn to paint people. As I run faster into the heart of art and my love for politics and law, I will learn to see the faces behind each page of cold policy text, the amazing innovation sketched in the tattered Constitution, and the progressiveness living in oak-paneled courts.

It won't be too far. I know that in a few years I will see a thousand more colors than I do today. Yet the most beautiful part about art is that there is no end. No matter how deep I penetrate its shimmering realms, the enigmatic caverns of wonder will stay.

REVIEW

The use of dialogue in Elizabeth's opening anecdote is particularly effective in drawing the attention of the reader while also conveying the sense of frustration Elizabeth felt in regard to her own artistic abilities. Her honesty concerning her feelings of inadequacy lend a candid tone to the essay and allow the reader to relate to her on a personal level. Furthermore, the author's willingness to describe a situation featuring her own shortcoming suggests a level of personal humility.

Elizabeth has done an effective job of using a short personal story to frame a larger discussion of her progression as an artist. Her ability to overcome her early feelings of frustration speak to her character and ability to persevere when faced with a challenge. More importantly, her language regarding colors and how they have altered the way she views the world convey a deep sense of passion for her favorite pastime. Elizabeth could have done without the tacked-on mentions of law and politics, as they distract from the main theme. Still, overall Elizabeth has written an interesting story that speaks both about her character and her love for painting.

—Matias Ferandel

RACHEL MYOUNG MOON

Hometown: Seoul, South Korea
High School: Private school, 400 students in graduating class
Ethnicity: Asian
Gender: Female
GPA: 4.0 out of 4.0
SAT: Reading 800, Math 800, Writing 720
ACT: n/a
SAT Subject Tests Taken: Mathematics Level 2, Chemistry, Physics
Extracurriculars: Research in greater horseshoe bats at Wildlife Ecology and Conservation Genomics Lab (Kangwon National University), Korean archery club founder and president, Dream and Act Volunteer Club vice president, mock trial
Awards: Ji In Yong award (given to the best student of the year), third prize in National Youth Korean Archery Championship, U.S. National Merit Scholarship semifinalist
Major: Integrative Biology

ESSAY

Language is not the sole domain of humans. Animals also talk, and over the last few years I have been fascinated by learning two new languages that even foreign language school students have never heard of. Studying animal languages is very different from learning Korean, Chinese, or Spanish. There are always dictionaries to refer to when I learn human languages, but when learning animal languages I don't have a google translator to spit out satisfactory answers. In fact, I have to use my own judgment, which combines my mind, heart, and instinct, to interpret what I hear.

Tree frogs, specifically Japanese tree frogs and Suweon tree frogs, use songs not just to express their amorous intentions but to survive. While these two species may look physically identical, they are sexually incompatible. So in order to lure the right female, male frogs sing serenades that are distinguishable from other species. Analyzing these serenades at an ecology lab with spectrograms and waveforms, I decoded every pulse of sound emitted by these ravenous tree frogs into patterns of numbers to let humans understand their lyrics.

Unlike frogs' mating songs, bats use language not only to communicate but also to navigate and locate insects at night. While flying, bats shoot out biosonar sounds and listen to the echoes that bounce off obstacles to grasp the world around them. Visualizing a world just with sound, I was enchanted by their invisible language when I studied the Greater Horseshoe bat's supersonic echolocation at a wildlife conservation lab. When bats cast nets of invisible words every millisecond during free flight and ziplining experiments, we captured and revealed their dialogue that had neither conjugations nor grammar.

After eavesdropping on treefrogs' and bats' conversations, I discovered that they use languages for survival. The language of the frogs exemplifies power—the stronger and bigger a frog is, the louder it can sing, scaring off all its prey and bravely exposing itself to predators. And for bats, their invisible language is their vision. They silently scream out for help and listen carefully as nature's echoes guide their path. In a sense, animals communicate with other species and with nature.

On the other hand, humans have developed esoteric words, convoluted sentences, and dialects to express their sophisticated ideas and feelings. This amazing evolution has, I believe, isolated us from nature. Now we prefer to live away from wildlife, tending to communicate only among other Homo sapiens sapiens through texts, tweets, and e-mails. Taking a page from Dr. DoLittle's pocket diction, I hope that my work helps us broaden our anthropocentric minds and understand animals who also share our biosphere. If our souls are reconnected with nature, maybe we could hear Mother Nature whisper some secrets about her mysteries that we are too wired or unaware to heed.

Early explorers boldly left the comforts of their homeland to learn the languages and traditions of other cultures. Due to their dedication, these self-taught bilinguals were able to bridge cultures and share values between different communities. In the same way, I want to take risks in learning to communicate with other species beyond human beings and become a multilingual biologist who connects human and animal realms. I wish to venture into the animal kingdom and become a pioneer in mastering and sharing nature's occult dialects with our species. When we finally learn to comprehend and harmonize with nature, we humans might become more humane.

REVIEW

Describing her study of animal languages was likely quite difficult for Rachel to express through other components of her application. Her essay brings to light this extremely unique academic interest while also depicting the relations and insight she draws between animal and human language.

Because it isn't a good idea to scholastically ramble in a college essay, Rachel instead weaves a story with a mixture of academic knowledge and self-reflection. Additionally, instead of writing about her interest in science or biology, she writes about a very specific scientific niche in which academic context is needed; similarly, she focused on providing just as much insight about the topic as she did about the academic details of the topic itself.

Rachel's powerful and articulate description of her interest captivates the reader. Her framing of animal language in humanistic terms, such as when she talks about bats' languages in terms of "conjunctions and grammar," makes the essay exceptional. She develops this comparison further near the end of the essay when she presents her insight about the disconnect between humans and animals and her future desires to reconnect the two. While the unique topic in itself was likely to grasp the audience's attention, Rachel's expressive reflections and explicit desire to continue studying the topic mesmerizes the reader even further.

—Annie Schugart

LAUREN SIERRA

Hometown: Brownsville, Texas, USA
High School: Public school, 555 students in graduating class
Ethnicity: Hispanic
Gender: Female
GPA: 3.8 out of 4.0
SAT: Reading 720, Math 650, Writing 690
ACT: 31
SAT Subject Tests Taken: n/a
Extracurriculars: Yearbook editor, newspaper editor, varsity tennis, Health Occupations Students of America national competitor and historian, National Honor Society vice president
Awards: National Champion in Health Occupations Students of America's Extemporaneous Writing Competition 2015, National Hispanic Recognition Scholar, Hugh O'Brian Youth Leadership nominee, South Texas Cotillion nominee
Major: Sociology

ESSAY

"What are you 'dying' of this time, Lauren?" This is the greeting I am met with every time I step foot into my pediatrician's office, which is much too often. If there were a rewards card for office visits, I would be a gold member. With every strange bump, slight cough, or nagging headache I get, I can only put my mind to rest by dragging my mother across town to get whatever is bothering me checked out. I am a hypochondriac by its very definition.

I have been afraid of everything pertaining to the medical field ever since the sight of a bloody scraped knee acquired on the third grade playground sent me into a collapse and convulsions. After an emergency room visit and what felt like hundreds of tests later, the doctors concluded that I was fine and that I had fainted simply out of fear. However, my 8-year-old self knew without any years of medical school education that there was actually something terribly wrong with me, and I would be on my deathbed before elementary graduation.

Throughout my childhood, the thought of everything from catching a disease to surgery made me feel nauseous. While most kids feared not finding a date to the middle school dance, I feared that a mosquito bite on my leg would lead me to be at death's door due to West Nile Virus within a week. I feared my life being cut short before I could even live it due to some freak disorder or disease, and I feared the state of eternal oblivion I would one day enter. A simple scraped knee led me to become incapacitated by the concept of sickness and essentially death. Despite all this, I still signed up for the medical career pathway all students at my high school typically take.

I managed to stomach my way through the first two years of textbook work and medical terminology memorization. However, I dreaded every second leading up to my junior year when I would have to perform clinical rotations around my local hospital. I viewed the hospital as the absolute embodiment of my hypochondriac-driven fears. I could not imagine myself thrust into the hospital environment once a week when I could not watch hospital shows on television without becoming anxious.

However, within the fluorescent halls of Valley Baptist Medical Center during my junior year, I learned the very definition of overcoming fear. Even though I was shaking in my scrubs, I was a spectator to everything from feeding tube installation to gastric surgery. I pushed thoughts of demise to the back of mind and pushed what little bravery I had to the front. My ears heard screams due to death and grief among the beeps of ICU machines but also heard the cries of joy and new beginnings in the women's pavilion. I saw death in the eyes of several patients, but I was also witness to recovery and new life. By the end of the year, I no longer dreaded my visits to the hospital but looked forward to what I would be exposed to.

I still become nervous every time I begin to feel the familiar tickle of a sore throat form behind my tongue, but I do not live a life paralyzed by the fear of something unavoidable. I will not spend my life being afraid of when the end of it will come and I like to consider myself oblivious to the oblivion which will one day overcome me. I no longer view death and disease with the same fear I acquired from my "life-threatening" third-grade incident. I view death and disease as old friends who will inevitably come knocking at my body's door someday, met with a warm embrace. Until then, I will keep bothering my doctor to make sure my friends stay away as long as they possibly can.

REVIEW

The ambiguous first line and lighthearted self-deprecation at the onset of this essay are a powerful combination. The author introduces herself by stating she is a hypochondriac, a defining characteristic that many would view as a major flaw. However, using vivid descriptive details and the hyperbole that plagued her childhood, the author redirects her reader to focus on a major obstacle. Rather than just telling her reader that she is persistent and hardworking, she shows herself as such by describing her experiences working in a hospital and illustrates her transformation and growth over time.

The author reveals her change in perspective at the end of the fifth paragraph and proves to her reader that she has truly grown. She is now open to new experiences and opportunities, a characteristic that entices admissions officers, who understand the abundance of new experiences a freshman in college will face.

The strength of this essay is in the descriptive language and the author's ability to show, rather than tell, her readers about her positive characteristics. An admissions officer reading this essay will appreciate the young woman who is not afraid to be outside of her comfort zone, is eager to embrace new experiences, and has shown that she is a very deep thinker with a lighthearted and positive attitude. The genuine and human qualities of this essay allow the reader to understand the young woman behind it, and as a result, admissions officers are drawn to the wit and spunk of a hypochondriac.

—Kathleen A. Cronin

II. INTELLECTUAL CURIOSITY

When you are applying to college, a baseline assumption is that you are continuing your education in order to learn from the professors and academic resources available at the schools you are applying to. Therefore, one way to impress admissions officers is to show them how you can contribute to the academic community in college. This allows the admissions officer to easily visualize how you will fit in at the school.

Some applicants have a strong and immediate passion for an area of study, while others find themselves slowly growing an appreciation for a subject over time. The one trait the students in this chapter all share is a strong commitment to learning and education. You will read about students exploring their intellectual capacity: a girl learns to appreciate ancient languages, a boy uses his own experience to teach younger children how to be effective public speakers, and an aspiring doctor performs brain surgery on a rat.

Tell admissions about how you've gone above and beyond in your academic explorations—and also show them you have the passion to continue this journey when you come to college.

DYLAN PARKER

Hometown: Pittsford, New York, US
High School: Public school, 250 students in graduating class
Ethnicity: White
Gender: Male
GPA: 96.22 out of 100
SAT: Reading 800, Math 760, Writing 770
ACT: 35
SAT Subject Tests Taken: Mathematics Level 1, Mathematics Level 2, Chemistry, U.S. History, World History
Extracurriculars: Model United Nations Secretary General, Quiz Bowl president, varsity tennis, Political Advocates president, National Honor Society secretary
Awards: National AP Scholar, National Merit Scholar, Frederick Douglass and Susan B. Anthony Award, NY Regents Scholarship, National Latin Exam Summa Cum Laude (4 consecutive years)
Major: Applied Math

ESSAY

$0x=0$.

This expression of mathematical mockery tells me that I know nothing; ambiguity pervades my world.

But I want to change that—by understanding everything.

I grant you, this is ambitious. But two summers ago I encountered economics. The study of decisions, economics empowers me to dissect situations like this: Yesterday I resolved to buy a binder (in addition to universal understanding, I burn for office supplies). After pacing the aisles of Staples for an embarrassingly long time, I whittled my options down to one blue and one red 3-inch Mead Five Star, identical in all but color. But, for whatever reason, the blue binder cost a dollar more. I bought it.

Irrational? I think not. Although not founded on binder functionality, my purchase would merit Spock's blessing because I assessed the marginal benefit of blueness as exceeding the marginal cost of $1. But if I'd pay a buck for blue, how about two? Three? I could find out by raising the blue binder's price until it isn't worth the extra charge— then I buy the red binder and spend my savings on a blue pen. With economics, I can measure anything.

Alas, understanding decisions isn't as easy as cataloging the value of everything to everyone, for we not only value the same factors differently, but also consult entirely disparate factors when making decisions. Other binder buyers may not just value color less than I do; they may not consider it at all.

Although well stocked in the confidence department, I concede that I, too, neglect relevant factors. So I'm irrational. Big whoop. But just as I cannot erect sturdy architecture from bendy straws (as calamitous collapses at Denny's have proved), I cannot construct a definable system from my irrational mind. My pantheon of omnipotence is starting to look more like a teepee.

I appeal to neuroscience for order. Armed with the study of mental processes, perhaps I can differentiate between factors I consider and ignore. But this is like knowing the verdict without knowing the law, the underlying scheme. To expose the system that delivers every judgment, I must know why I attended to some factors and not others.

I petition psychology for inspiration. Experience could condition me to jettison the trivial to focus on the essential. This seems reasonable. If I am equally competent with Staples and Office Depot binders, I won't consider that when making my purchase. But how do I quantify the influence of my past?

I implore mathematics for a solution. Or perhaps computer science could better cipher the code of humankind. Or has history guarded the truth all along?

It may be all of the above! Can a neuroscience-inspired computer use economic models for decision theory, tweaked with mathematically rendered psychoanalytic principles, to map my brain by analyzing past decisions? Can I solve my brain as an infinite system of variables with each past decision as an equation that brings me a step closer to isolating the unknowns? Can I then peer into history with complete comprehension? Can I apply the same method to the future? Can I know the future?

I don't see why not. But let's leave Doc and Marty McFly and briefly revisit the present.

My world exists in chaos. It is a puzzle whose pieces are strewn across the floor, awaiting assembly. So every morning I open my books and battle for knowledge, assaulting the palisades of ambiguity so that one night when I close my books I will see the world as I see economics—I will *understand*.

REVIEW

Dylan's essay uncovers his desire to understand everything. What makes it memorable is the moment at Staples when Dylan struggled to decide which binder to buy. Dylan was able to discuss how his economics education changed his way of thinking within this anecdote. It is also very well-structured; each paragraph further exemplifies the writer's curiosity and thirst for knowledge—one little situation in Staples compels him to wonder how he can understand the whole of history. This style allows the essay to build momentum, and Dylan successfully maintains it until the end.

This essay could have benefitted from jumping straight into the Staples scene. Readers tend to be more interested in something they can visualize and connect with. Fortunately, Dylan includes this scene close to the start of the essay to offset the mathematical jargon of the first lines. He also succeeds by peppering humorous thoughts and pop culture references in parentheses throughout the essay, which prevents the tone from being pretentious.

The final paragraph is a meaningful rumination on the rhetorical questions Dylan asks throughout the essay. It fully establishes the writer as a curious discoverer who is forever in pursuit of knowledge.

—Leah S. Yared

SHERIDAN MARSH

Hometown: Glendale, California, USA
High School: Private all-female school, 47 students in graduating class
Ethnicity: Asian and Black
Gender: Female
GPA: 4.2 out of 4.0
SAT: n/a
ACT: 33
SAT Subject Tests Taken: Physics, Literature, U.S. History
Extracurriculars: Chamber orchestra—first violin, creative writing, varsity swimming, club swimming
Awards: Departmental honors: English, Latin, history; member of Cum Laude Society, first-place winner in Fox Classics Writing Contest hosted by Monmouth College
Major: Undecided

ESSAY

I'm better at writing other people's stories than I am at writing my own. You could ask me to write a twenty-page story about a scrawny Roman soldier who cries during battle, and I could do it easily (and I have), but if you asked me to write a few words about myself, I'd be hard pressed to give you any. I live in worlds that aren't my own and spend my days walking through classical Greece or attending Liszt concerts in busy nineteenth-century Paris all while sitting quietly at my desk with my elbow propped up on a math textbook. I've seen Achilles fight on the Trojan beach; I've laughed at Mozart cracking crude jokes among a flurry of sheet music and wine. I'll write all of these things for you before I write about myself, because the things I see in my mind's eye are more compelling than real life. I write because it allows me to forget myself, to lose myself in cobblestone streets so tangible that I bump into French revolutionaries who shout "Vive la liberté" as I shove by, only to discover upon glancing in the mirror that I am in fact a French revolutionary myself, with a slightly tattered cockade pinned to my lapel. My name isn't Sheridan; in fact, it's Antoine, and I have a nearly unrivaled dedication to the Republic.

In truth, I write because I found myself weak in the face of my reality. My life isn't particularly difficult or tragic, but I'm sensitive, and I sometimes feel out of place in my social world. Though I have friends that I cherish, I've often felt that I've been on the outside, be it because of my African American roots or simply the fact that our interests don't quite line up, but year after year of the same isolating experience left me wanting escape, and I found myself wondering in history class, wandering the halls of Versailles in my mind with Louis XIV or reciting poetry with the Roman emperor Augustus. These places were far away from the lunch table, far away from social dramas and empty Kleenex boxes, but yet, they were familiar enough to be comfortable. When I wrote my little twenty-page (and slightly historically inaccurate) story about a scrawny Roman soldier, Crescentius Avitus, I was a sophomore who had no idea what battle was like. I didn't know how to jab someone with a spear or how to march in a Roman legion, but I did know what it was like to feel inadequate and what it was like to feel alone. In unfamiliar social situations, I tensed up the way Crescentius did as he gripped his sword and shield, I shivered the way he did under his clattering helmet. As I wrote, I got lost in Crescentius' world through my connection with his humanity. My love for history and my love for writing stem from my realization that history was made of people who cried the way I cried, laughed the way I laughed. I could forget myself because I wasn't the only one to feel the way that I felt. I doubt that the French revolutionaries I bumped into earlier experienced anger that was different from the anger that I experienced. I write about others because humanity isn't an individual experience, and allowing yourself to experience the burden of humanity through sharing it with others is far easier than trying to understand it by yourself. This exchange goes both ways, and I use it to gain qualities that I lack. I am not particularly confident, but Antoine is. Through him, I learn to greet adversity with a grin and a fire; I learn to treat the lunch table like he would treat the podium at the National Convention, and through my experience in his world, I know how to hold my head high and fearlessly.

REVIEW

Sheridan begins by introducing us to her curious relationship with writing: While she seems secure in her ability to fictionalize history, she also expresses some reserve about using individual life experiences as subject matter. It's a smart admission to make, especially in response to a prompt that requires her to engage in that which she most fears: self-disclosure.

Perhaps the most powerful testament to Sheridan's appreciation of narrative is her own crisp prose. Her grasp of language imbues the essay with a lyrical and rhythmic energy. Though her declarations sometimes veer on the fanciful and hyperbolic, they convince the reader of her earnest wit and reveal details—albeit passing ones—about personal difficulties. Using historical places and events—like Versailles and the National Convention—as storytelling devices, Sheridan casts herself as a socially anxious protagonist who derives courage from, and solace in, the past.

Sheridan also uses an endearing, even self-effacing, kind of humor that convinces readers of her authenticity. By describing her twenty-page story about the "scrawny" Crescentius Avitus as "little"—and admitting, too, that it was "slightly historically inaccurate"—she shows a balanced perspective. While relaying her emotions with a measure of gravity, Sheridan knows not to take herself, or her work, *too* seriously; at the end of the day, after all, she inhabits a reality filled with "empty Kleenex boxes" and not bloodied spears.

Overall, Sheridan builds to a potent conclusion: Empathy, we learn, drives her passion for stories—both reading, and writing, them. Citing a desire to relate to people as her primary motivation, Sheridan appears a sympathetic and likable character: an ideal addition, in short, for a student body.

—Aisha Bhoori

ATHENA BRAUN

Hometown: Philadelphia, Pennsylvania, USA
High School: Private Quaker school, 56 students in graduating class
Ethnicity: Hispanic
Gender: Female
GPA: 4.2 out of 4.0
SAT: Reading 750, Math 660, Writing 790
ACT: n/a
SAT Subject Tests Taken: U.S. History, French, Spanish
Extracurriculars: Yearbook editor in chief, student government representative, varsity crew captain, Vegetarian Club leader
Awards: National Hispanic Scholar Award, high school high honors, language award
Major: Linguistics

ESSAY

Languages have played a central role in my life. I have studied a variety of languages, to varying degrees, but always in the name of my greater goal, which is to understand people—to truly comprehend what lies beneath the surface: How does a culture conceive of itself? What can we learn about how the Japanese based on formality of address? What can be said about the Germans, whose language requires the verb appear at the end of a sentence? Maybe not much, but without knowledge of the language, the possibility of real understanding is impaired. My interest in linguistics—and psychology as well—derives from this belief: there is an underlying structure to all language, and through the study and comprehension of this structure, there can be a mutual understanding.

Beyond the underlying structure, words themselves have a deep and rich history, and their usage is a form of beauty in itself. It was my father who opened my eye to this truth—who taught me to love words for their stories and to appreciate etymology. It began as a friendly contest between us, but for me, appreciation soon became full-fledged adoration that was only encouraged by my study of Latin. I began drawing connections I had previously missed between words I use every day, and I found myself spending hours in front of the computer looking for sites to aid me in my discoveries. One of my favorite discoveries (and an apt one to share with you) is the word *hedera*.

I happened upon *hedera* when I noticed the similarity among the words *apprehend*, *aprender*, and *apprendre*, "to learn" in Spanish and French, respectively. It was clear, judging by the orthography and definitions, that these words shared a Latin root, but in my studies, never had I come across such a word. Next thing I knew, I had the following on my hands: apprentice, comprehend, prehensile, apprehensive—a list of seemingly unrelated words—and only more questions. What relationship exists between one who is learning a trade and a sense of foreboding? The answer lay within the etymologies, which led to *hedera*, the Latin word for ivy. Once suffixes had been stripped away, the remaining word was always *-hendere*. Alone, the word means virtually nothing; it was contrived from *hedera* as a verb form to convey a sense of grasping. What better to do so than ivy, a plant known for its tenacity? I could not help but admire the ivy which had embedded itself into the foundations of language.

Language is all about meaning and understanding, but to grasp the true meaning of language, one must look beyond the surface of the sentence to the structure, and even beyond that to the meaning and histories of the words themselves. Language, therefore, is my passion because it is the study of understanding.

REVIEW

The strength of Athena's essay lies, unsurprisingly, in her adept use of language to string together sentences as nicely written as they are communicative. Athena's writing is uncharacteristically advanced for her age: It is free of the attempts at poetic flourish that often appear in personal statements and manages to showcase her extensive vocabulary without using ten-dollar words. As Athena puts forward, words and language are the tools she commands best; her essay is proof of this.

As for its content, this essay successfully exhibits its author's intellectual curiosity by parsing through the reasons why she loves linguistics and then demonstrating her learning process by parsing an actual word. And yet, this exercise causes the writer to stray from her initial discussion of how linguistics helps her better understand cultures and people, a wildly intriguing concept that ultimately doesn't get much airtime here.

Beyond that, this essay could exhibit more about its author as an individual. Though Athena alludes to a playful relationship with her father, this is all we get in the way of a glimpse into her personality. At 475 words, this essay is well under the 650-word limit. A more colorful introduction, some insight into how Athena's love of linguistics shapes her interactions with others, or a more personal conclusion could liven up what is already a sound argument for the writer's keen intellect.

—Lily K. Calcagnini

BRIAN YU

Hometown: Danville, California, USA
High School: Public school, 598 students in graduating class
Ethnicity: Asian
Gender: Male
GPA: 4.0 out of 4.0
SAT: Reading 800, Math 800, Writing 800
ACT: n/a
SAT Subject Tests Taken: Mathematics Level 2, Biology E/M, Chemistry, U.S. History, World History
Extracurriculars: Speech and debate team president, Science Alliance president, martial arts instructor, National Honor Society vice president
Awards: Speech and Debate National Champion in United States Extemporaneous Speaking (2015), California Speech and Debate State Champion in United States Extemporaneous Speaking (2013, 2014, and 2015), US Presidential Scholars semifinalist, National Merit Scholar finalist
Major: Computer Science and Linguistics

ESSAY

The summer after my freshman year, I found myself in an old classroom holding a blue dry-erase marker, realizing what should have been obvious: I had no idea how to be a teacher. As an active speech and debate competitor, I was chosen as a volunteer instructor for an elementary public speaking camp hosted by my high school. For the first time, I would have the opportunity to experience the classroom from the other side of the teacher's desk. My responsibility was simple: in two weeks, take sixteen fifth graders and turn them into confident, persuasive speakers.

I walked into class the first morning, enthusiastically looking forward to the opportunity to share my knowledge, experiences, and stories. I was hoping for motivated kids, eager to learn, attentive to my every word.

Instead, I got Spencer, who thought class was a good time to train his basketball skills by tossing crumpled speeches into the trash can from afar. I got Monica, who refused to speak, and I got James, who didn't understand the difference between "voice projection" and "screaming." I got London, who enjoyed doodling on her desk with permanent marker, and I got Arnav, who thought I wouldn't notice him playing Angry Birds all day. The only questions I got were "When's lunch break?" and "Why are you giving us homework?" and the only time I got my students to raise their hands was when I asked "How many of you are only here because your parents forced you?"

Just ten minutes into class, two things hit me: Spencer's crumpled paper basketball, and the realization that teaching was *hard*.

When I was younger, I thought a good teacher was one that gave high-fives after class. Later, of course, I knew it was far more complicated than that. I thought about teachers I admired and their memorable qualities. They were knowledgeable, enthusiastic, and inspiring. Their classes were always fun, and they always taught me something.

There was plenty I wanted to teach, from metaphors to logical fallacies. But most importantly, I wanted my students to enjoy public speaking, to love giving speeches as much as I did. And that's when I realized the most important quality of my favorite teachers: passion. They loved their subject and passed that love on to their students. While it wouldn't be easy, I wanted to do the same.

Every day for two weeks, I searched for creative ways to inspire and teach my students. I helped London speak on her love for art; I had Arnav debate about cell phones policies in schools. And by the end of the camp, I realized that my sixteen students all saw me not as a high school student, but as a teacher. I took their questions, shared my enthusiasm, and by the time camp was over, they weren't just learning, but enjoying learning.

I was on the other side of the teacher's desk, but I hadn't stopped learning. Each day, I was learning how to communicate more effectively, how to deal with new challenges and circumstances, and how to be a better teacher. I once thought that being an adult meant knowing all the answers. But in reality, adults, even teachers, constantly have more to learn. I made the transition away from being a child during those weeks, but I did not and would not transition away from being a learner.

When class ended each afternoon, I would cap my blue dry-erase marker, give high-fives to the students as they walked out the door, and watch as their parents picked them up. I was confident that when my students were asked the inevitable questions of "Did you learn something today?" and "Did you have fun?" their answers would be a resounding yes. And even as their teacher, I learned and had fun too.

REVIEW

Brian's choice of subject matter is carefully considered: he doesn't attempt to dazzle us with any flashy exploits or overwhelm us with the breadth and depth of his achievements. Instead, he chooses a simple success story, of his experience working with kids at a public speaking camp, that highlights his personal growth.

The story has a complete narrative arc, with a definite beginning, middle, and end. Brian describes a distinct set of opinions that characterize each phase of his short teaching career, illustrated with colorful descriptions of typical moments for each. There are also certain symmetries between the beginning and end (the blue marker, for example) that leave the reader with a sense of finality and satisfaction. In addition, Brian's voice throughout the story is phenomenal. His humor feels natural, and he's able to make the reader aware of his positive qualities without bragging or posturing; he shows them to us, through the story and through his subject, rather than loudly announcing them. His writing is confident and clear and doesn't distract at all from the content of the essay.

It's important to note that even though Brian's story depicts a success, a good college essay need not end in triumph. If you try to create a victory where there isn't really one, you run the risk of sounding insincere. You have plenty of other places to list your accomplishments!

—Adriano Iqbal, Trevor Levin, and Thomas Westbrook

RONNI CUCCIA

Hometown: Covina, California, USA
High School: Public school, 450 students in graduating class
Ethnicity: White
Gender: Female
GPA: 4.0 out of 4.0
SAT: Reading 680, Math 660, Writing 730
ACT: n/a
SAT Subject Tests Taken: Biology E/M, Literature
Extracurriculars: Club soccer captain, newspaper sports editor, National Honor Society president, California Scholarship Federation president, National Science Bowl captain
Awards: All-Academic Team for Palomares League for soccer, National Hispanic Scholar, AP Scholar, Co-Student-Athlete of the Year, second team all Palomares League, valedictorian
Major: Sociology

ESSAY

Canvass the people who know me—friends, family, teammates—and I'm certain they would all agree on one description of me. I'm a good student. I'd offer that label up myself.

I know that's fairly boring, but I just turned 18. There's still so much I don't know or haven't experienced. Future selves (author? professor? reality TV star?) are yet to come. But one thing I do know with certainty is that being a good student is not just about getting good grades.

Through ninth grade, I measured myself in A's. School was a place where I spent seven hours a day, aching for the day to end. I was motivated to get those A's only because my parents wanted me to. However, I didn't care. Liberated by the school bell, I would turn off my brain and focus on other things: friends, sports, and the contents of the DVR. Nothing in a classroom had ever inspired me to do much more than my homework.

Then I took AP world history with Mr. Stratton. I started out terrified: this was my first AP class. I anticipated challenging material and copious homework, and yes, those things did happen. But I didn't mind it: I trusted my teacher. I even started to worry less about the test in May. What I discovered—happily—was the sheer joy of learning.

"What's going to make you successful in the future are hard work, passion, and curiosity—not the numbers one to five," Mr. Stratton told us. I remember the words verbatim because I recorded his speech to the class the day before the AP exam. That was how crazily excited I was about this class.

He was an amazing and, yes, life-changing teacher. He showed a "grade junkie" (a common term of his) like myself that it's not about the tests or scores. Questions. Discovery. Knowledge. These are the things that actually matter.

I still spout off information from AP World—especially from chapter 29: "The French Revolution." I've often compared the hierarchies of my own high school to the stratified society of France. (Plans for a Basketball Court Oath—we don't have tennis courts, alas—have yet to materialize.)

My new enthusiasm extended to all my classes and activities. Everything had something to offer—even Physics. I found my identity as a good student, embracing those principles of hard work, passion, and curiosity. Now I cherish all of my hours at school wholeheartedly, from pep rallies to the soccer field, from the science lab to the newspaper room. Furthermore, I seek to educate myself outside the syllabus, reading Sylvia Plath or watching YouTube videos on history. I want to be a good student of life.

I find knowledge satisfying when it provides perspective on the state of the world. History, literature, science, politics, Spanish—every course gives me a greater understanding of how people behave, how the world works, why things are the way they are. (And also prepares me, I hope, to change the world in my own ways in the future.) Mr. Stratton taught us about the Age of Enlightenment—and his class was itself a time of enlightenment for me.

I am proof that good students are made by good teachers. I am grateful to Mr. Stratton and every other teacher I have had who has changed me, inspired me, informed me, and yes, graded me. This passion for learning they have ignited in me will continue to burn through my college years—a new Age of Enlightenment.

I cannot help but browse college course descriptions, eager to embark on new adventures of learning. I know I am a good student—and I hope to be one for the rest of my life.

REVIEW

In this essay, Ronni presents herself sincerely and openly. The lighthearted introduction effectively establishes the fact that she will be talking about the academic side of her life without sounding pretentious or full of herself. She does an excellent job of integrating her academic life and her life outside of school, reminding the reader that she is, indeed, only eighteen years old. Most importantly, she is able to briefly share an anecdote about an experience that was important to her and use it to explain other parts of her life. Without beating the reader over the head, she reminds us that she plays soccer, enjoys science, and writes for the newspaper. The inclusion of these activities does not sound like a readout of her résumé but deftly accomplishes the same effect. A good college essay helps build a narrative around your candidacy, so including many different parts of your life is wise. Her inclusion of extracurricular activities and topics she is interested in helps build that narrative.

When writing about academics as Ronni does here, it is important to keep in mind that the purpose of your essay is not to tell a college that you are smart. That's what your grades and test scores are for. The purpose of the essay is to share your authentic self with a college in a way that is simply impossible on a résumé. Ronni walks that line well here. This essay is also a strong reminder of the fact that colleges admit actual high school students. Applicants to selective colleges are often tempted to write an essay filled with pretentious words, confusing diction, and a tone of arrogant falsified erudition. Avoid this urge, just as Ronni avoided it. Take a few minutes and read your essay out loud. Do you recognize your own voice in your words? If you don't hear your voice, how will an admission officer? This essay is strong because Ronni's voice shines through.

—Ryan O'Meara

BETH YOUNG

Hometown: Belmont, Massachusetts, USA
High School: Public school, 306 students in graduating class
Ethnicity: Asian
Gender: Female
GPA: 3.95 out of 4.0
SAT: n/a
ACT: n/a
SAT Subject Tests Taken: n/a
Extracurriculars: Model United Nations president, Working to Help the Homeless president, Belmontian (community service club) secretary, Speech and Debate founder and president
Awards: AP National Scholar, Belmont High School Book Award, Belmont Latin Book Award, high honor roll
Major: Psychology

ESSAY

"Ut Italiam laeti Latiumque petamus"*

"Beth, would you mind reading the next few lines and translating them for us?"

The professor glanced at me, a kind glimmer in his bespectacled eyes. I gulped. I was in a classroom of eighteen, five of whom were high school Latin teachers. And *I* was supposed to recite and

---

*Translation: so that we, happy, might seek Italy and Latium.

translate Livy's *Ab Urbe Condita*—with elisions! After fumbling through a few words and mistaking a verb for a noun, I finished the first sentence. I skimmed the second line, looking for the main verb. *Singular.* I searched for a singular noun and pieced the two together. Then, I noticed an accusative and added it as a direct object. As I continued, a burst of exhilaration shot through my body. My eyes darted across the page, finding a verb, a noun, and objects. I reached the end of the passage and grinned, relief pulsing in my veins.

"Very good!" The professor beamed at me before selecting his next victim.

A few months ago, I never would have imagined myself sitting in Harvard's Boylston Hall this summer for six hours a week, cherishing the ancient literature of Rome. Even though the professor decided I was eligible for the course despite not taking the prerequisite, I was still nervous. I worked hard in the class, and it reminded just how much I love the language.

Translating has always given me great pleasure and great pain. It is much like completing a jigsaw puzzle. First, I notice words that form the backbone of the sentence: the subject and the main verb. This is the border of my puzzle. Next, I look for phrases that connect the entire clause—does this adjective match this noun? Does this puzzle piece have the right shape? The middle of the sentence is the trickiest, full of convoluted dependent clauses, pieces colored ambiguously and with curves and edges on all four sides. I am sometimes tangled in the syntax, one of the worst feelings in the world. After analyzing every word, I try to rearrange the pieces so they fit together. When they finally do, I am filled with a satisfaction like no other. Translating forces me to rattle my brain, looking for grammatical rules hidden in my mind's nooks and crannies. It pushes my intellectual boundaries. No other language is as precise, using inflection to express gender, number, and case in just one word. When I pull apart a sentence, I am simultaneously divulging the secrets of an ancient civilization. Renowned scholars are telling the stories of their time through these words! No other language is as meticulous. Every line follows the same meter and the arrangement of every word is with a purpose. The story of Pyramus and Thisbe includes a sentence where the word "wall" is placed between the words "Pyramus" and "Thisbe" to visually show the lovers' separation. Translating is like life itself; the words are not in logical order. One cannot expect the subject of a sentence to appear at the beginning of a clause, just like one cannot plan the chronology of life. Like the delayed verb, we do not always know what is happening in our lives; we just know it *is* happening. When translating, we notice the nouns, the adjectives and the conjunctions just like we see the people, senses, and connections of our lives. However, we often do not know what we are doing and ask ourselves an age-old question: Why are we here? Perhaps we are here to learn, to teach, to help, to serve, to lead, or just to live. We travel through life to decide what our purpose is, and it is that suspense and our unknown destinies that make the journey so irresistibly beautiful. I feel that same suspense and unknown when I translate, because I am beautifully struggling to unlock a past I know very little of. It is unbelievably exhilarating.

Thus, I question why others consider Latin a dead language. It is alive in all of the Western world. The Romance languages of French, Spanish, and Italian all have Latin origins. Without Latin, I would not be able to write this essay! It is alive in the stories it tells. You may see an apple and associate it with orchards, juice, pie, and fall. When I see an apple, I think of the apple of discord thrown by Eris that ultimately caused the Trojan War. This event, albeit destructive and terrifying, leads to the flight of Aeneas and eventually, his founding of Rome.

I study Latin for its rewarding return, incredible precision, intellectual challenge, rich history and culture, and deep influence on our world. I study Latin to show others how beautiful it is, to encourage the world that it should be valued. I study Latin to lead our society, like Aeneas did, toward a new city, a new dawn where everyone appreciates a mental trial of wits, everyone marvels at a vibrant past, and no one wonders whether Latin is dead or not.

REVIEW

What I found most striking about Beth's essay was not the fact that she was taking a class alongside high school Latin teachers, or that she was taking a summer class at Harvard. Rather, it was how in-depth Beth went into her thought process when translating Latin. It became clear from the vivid detail with which she described her translating process that she takes it rather seriously, and it is always a pleasure to read application essays that make such passion clear.

That said, there are times where Beth's writing appears to deliberately make something engaging when there is no need. For example, "One cannot expect the subject of a sentence to appear at the beginning of a clause, just like one cannot plan the chronology of life" seemed to be an intentionally poetic sentence made to fit Beth's claim that "translating is like life itself." Overall, the simile works, but you should not feel forced to make dramatic claims in your essay. If you write about something that you are passionate about, that should naturally become clear in the way you write.

—M. Hanl Park

HENRY SHAH

Hometown: Philadelphia, Pennsylvania, USA
High School: Private Quaker school, 84 students in graduating class
Ethnicity: Biracial
Gender: Male
GPA: 3.93 out of 4.0
SAT: Reading 800, Math 700, Writing 770
ACT: n/a
SAT Subject Tests Taken: U.S. History, World History
Extracurriculars: Cross country / indoor track / outdoor track captain, newspaper editor in chief, literary magazine editor, Monday Series—speaking series and publication founder and editor, Student Religious Life Committee chair, Student Council, Obama 2012 campaign organizer
Awards: Award as top community organizer in country for the Obama 2012 campaign; State champion in cross country, 4 years in a row
Major: History and Literature

ESSAY

When I broke the news to my volunteer team, we were in a church basement, cleaning up after the final event of the summer. I tried to downplay it. I nudged Ms. Diana, the neighborhood leader, in the shoulder, and said, "Guess what I'll be doing next Wednesday—having lunch with the president." Her face blazed with a kilowatt smile. Before I could slow her down, she shouted, "Henry's meeting President Obama next week."

Eldred dropped his broom, Ms. Sheila left the cups scattered on the floor, and all the others came running over and fusilladed me with questions. Yes, the campaign had chosen me from all the other summer organizers. Yes, I would bring photos for everyone. And yes, we had the strongest team by the numbers—total calls, knocks, voters registered, and events—in the country.

I felt guilty that only I could go and told them so. "I wish that I could bring you all with me. You made nearly all of the calls, brought your friends and family along, and made this what it is. I've just been here to facilitate." The others good-naturedly shouted me down. Then Ms. Melva spoke up. Her words were pressed out against the heaving of her respirator. "Henry, don't feel bad. You'll bring us wherever you go in your pocket. Just pull us out when you meet Barack."

For a long time, I was perplexed by her advice. Then I thought back to the exercise that we employed before any volunteer activity. We sat in a circle and gave our reasons for being in the room, willing to work with the campaign. That way, when it came time to make our "hard ask" on the phones, we would be supported by personal conviction and shared purpose. The "hard ask" is the Obama campaign's tactic for garnering support or a commitment to volunteer, moving from values and idealism to specific action.

In my work on the campaign, I am reminded of my cross-country coach, Rob. Before every single race, from petty league meets to national championships, Rob taps the spot on his thigh where a pocket would be. We look at our teammates who are lining up with us and tap the same spot. Coach Rob is reminding us, and we're reminding each other, that we carry "the bastard" in our pockets with us throughout the race. "The bastard in your pocket" is a metaphor for the sum of our efforts to succeed as runners. "The bastard" exists as a sort of Platonic ideal form of the high school cross-country runner, melded from accrued mileage and mental conditioning. My goal in a race is to take this ideal form and to transform it into a reality that lives on the course.

I want an education that fills my pockets. And, perhaps more importantly, an education that prompts hard asks, that demands us to use "the bastard" and that uses the compounded experiences of a group for a single purpose.

REVIEW

Through the two examples of his volunteer work and cross-country experience, Henry is able to depict a nuanced and sophisticated understanding of leadership and a profound dedication to teamwork.

In the opening paragraphs, he describes the moment in which he related news of an invitation to meet the president to his volunteer team. The moment is shown as the culmination of all of Henry's efforts as a summer organizer for the Obama campaign. The mention of the invitation serves as a validation of demonstrable and impressive leadership; further, the reference to members of his team by name displays that his work was meaningful and personal.

Throughout the essay, Henry reveals his passion for forming and being a part of a community as both a goal in itself and as a way to achieve success for the team. This is a point he elaborates upon in his reference to "the bastard in your pocket," which he presents as an ideal that can be transformed into action in order to achieve success. An allusion to the words of his cross-country coach, he uses this example to expand upon his views toward community and lived experience. He talks about both action and intention, emphasizing his own success in transforming beliefs and ideas into tangible results. The last paragraph in Henry's essay serves as a succinct but powerful conclusion, one that links the kind of educational experience he seeks with his determined, goal-actualizing mentality.

—Mahnoor Ali

DEEPIKA KURUP

Hometown: Nashua, New Hampshire, USA
High School: Public school, 500 students in graduating class
Ethnicity: Asian
Gender: Female
GPA: 4.0 out of 4.0
SAT: Reading 750, Math 800, Writing 730
ACT: n/a
SAT Subject Tests Taken: Mathematics Level 2, Biology E/M, Chemistry
Extracurriculars: National Honors Society, Math Honors Society, varsity math team, Science Bowl captain and founder
Awards: America's Top Young Scientist, *Forbes* 30 Under 30, Stockholm Junior Water Prize national winner, ISEF second Grand Award
Major: Neurobiology

ESSAY

I first performed brain surgery before I learned how to drive. I vividly remember guiding a slender, metal scalpel and the thin trail of red that followed. Before I made my next incision, I took a look at my patient, a Sprague Dawley rat, to make sure he was still breathing. Then came the trickiest part: drilling a hole just deep enough to pierce the skull, while saving the brain beneath it from harm. With one accidental slip of the hand, I could sever this animal's brain and prevent it from ever awakening. However, despite this responsibility placed on my hands, I felt perfectly confident and successfully executed the surgery.

My hands-on experience of performing brain surgery was part of my research internship with the National Institutes of Health Summer Internship Program (NIH SIP). In order to academically prepare myself for this competitive program, I started taking advanced placement science and math courses ahead of my peers, in my first two years of high school. After contacting several principal investigators at the National Institute of Neurological Disorders and Stroke (NINDS), a division within the NIH, I was accepted by Dr. Judith Walters, whose research focuses on Parkinson's disease.

Parkinson's disease is a neurodegenerative disorder that is characterized by rigidity and a lack of motor coordination. Slight unsteadiness gradually creeps into the patient until they are unable to perform simple tasks such as brushing their teeth or buttoning their shirt. The current standard treatment for Parkinson's disease is a drug called levodopa. While levodopa is effective for initial therapy, prolonged treatment often leads to the development of abnormal involuntary movements. At the NIH, I conducted research to better understand the mechanisms underlying the development of these involuntary movements. The hemiparkinsonian Sprague Dawley rat (a rat with half of its brain affected by the disease) was used as an animal model. The results of my research and future investigations in this area may contribute to improved treatment methods for Parkinson's disease patients.

As one of the youngest researchers at the NIH, I felt privileged to be working alongside graduate students and postdoctoral fellows who had an extensive knowledge of the subject. Toward the end of my internship, I finished compiling results for my final poster presentation. I was honored to receive the Exceptional Summer Student Award for my work titled "The Relationship between Spiking Activity and High Gamma Oscillations in the Ventral Medial Thalamus during L-dopa-induced Dyskinesia." My presentation was one of the top three of all NINDS interns' projects, so the following day I was selected to deliver a lecture to a large audience of NIH researchers and fellow interns. On my last day at the NIH, I was thrilled to learn that the results of my research may contribute to a future journal paper.

For me, everything from the task of reading scientific papers on neurology, to the quest of sorting through hundreds of neurological recordings, to the thrill of performing brain surgery has been gratifying. My enriching experience at the NIH gave me a profound appreciation for medical research, and the confidence that we will soon find cures for many neurological disorders.

REVIEW

While research internships are fairly common essay topics, Deepika's account of her experience stands out because of the balance she strikes between explanation, entertainment, and self-reflection.

In her opening sentence, she juxtaposes performing brain surgery and learning to drive, emphasizing the impressiveness of her accomplishment for her age without sounding arrogant. She uses the shock-and-awe factor of brain surgery to her advantage by not revealing her patient—a rat—until later in the paragraph. She effectively builds suspense and then transitions into a useful explanation of her internship.

Deepika conveys her commitment to academics and research by describing how she took AP courses early in high school and personally contacted researchers and professors at the NIH. She shows her initiative and academic achievements without listing them like a résumé.

While some background about her research is necessary, her explanation of Parkinson's is a bit too long—it pulls the reader's focus away from Deepika. The essay could have been even more effective if she had talked more specifically about what she actually did or any particular challenges she faced.

In her final paragraphs, Deepika reflects on how this opportunity allowed her to learn from others, contribute to pressing medical inquiries, and affirm her passion for medical research. A final sentence about what she hopes to do in the future or how the experience has influenced her goals for college could have made her essay even stronger.

—Brittany Ellis

YEHONG ZHU

Hometown: Newnan, Georgia, USA
High School: Public school, 597 students in graduating class
Ethnicity: Asian
Gender: Female
GPA: 4.0 out of 4.0
SAT: Reading 800, Math 800, Writing 800
ACT: n/a
SAT Subject Tests Taken: U.S. History, Literature
Extracurriculars: Varsity Academic Bowl cocaptain; varsity lacrosse four year letterman, Chess Club president; Distinguished Young Women of Georgia 2014; Distinguished Young Women of Coweta County; Centre Strings Orchestra, first violin
Awards: U.S. Presidential Scholars semifinalist, National Merit Scholar, National AP Scholar, Outstanding Georgia Citizen, Georgia Region 3B STAR Student
Major: Philosophy and Government

ESSAY

I was in 9th grade the first time I stumbled upon a copy of *Newsweek*. What caught my eye was its trademark title: white type, red highlight, a connotation that stories of great consequence lay beneath. Such bold lettering gave me a moment's pause, and I was prompted to leaf through its glossy pages.

To my surprise, I was instantly hooked.

A new world unfolded before me. Biting social commentary. World conflicts that weren't dumbed down. Piquant reviews of best-selling books, controversial exposés of political figures, tantalizing tidbits on pop culture, full-page spreads of photographs.

And the prose was elegant, sharp, *mesmerizing*. It radiated sophistication and IQ. As I scanned the credentials of the authors, my only thought was, *wow*. The articles were written by worldly, ambitious people who were experts in their fields, people with PhDs and MBAs from world-class institutions, people who could write brilliantly, who got paid to give their opinions, who walked with a purpose and ran in the direction of their dreams. People I knew—then and there—I'd like to one day become.

This is what education looks like, I told myself. I was young, I was impressionable. Like a child standing on the outside of a candy store, nose pressed against the glass, I hungered to be a part of that cerebral adult world. So I read that magazine from cover to cover. Twice. And with each turn of the page I felt my small-town naïveté break into smaller and smaller pieces. I remember that day as an incredibly humbling experience. I had an awkward, self-conscious epiphany: that I actually knew next to nothing about the world. There I was, cream of the crop of my middle school, fourteen years of "smart" outwitted by a thin volume of paper. I was used to feeling gifted, to getting gold stickers and good grades, to acing every elementary examination placed in front of my cocky #2 pencil.

I wasn't used to feeling like I'd been living in the Dark Ages.

At the same time, however, I struggled with another realization, one that was difficult for me to define. I felt . . . *liberated*. I felt as though I had taken a breath of fresh air and found it to be bracing and delicious, like it was the first breath I'd ever taken, and I'd never known that air was so sweet.

Talk about a paradigm shift: somehow, reading *Newsweek* had rekindled my natural intellectual curiosity; it had, briefly, filled a hole in my soul that I didn't know existed.

It had also sparked something within me—a hint of defiance, a refusal to accept complacency. One taste of forbidden fruit, and I knew I could never go back.

Although reading a news magazine seemed like a nonevent at the time, in retrospect it was one of the defining moments of my adolescence. That seemingly unextraordinary day set a lot of subsequent days in motion—days when I would push my limitations, jump a little higher, venture out of my comfort zone and into unfamiliar territory, days when I would fail over and over again only to succeed when I least expected it, days when I would build my dreams from scratch, watch them fall down, then build them back up again, and before I knew it, the days bled into years, and this was my life.

At 14, I'd caught a glimpse of where the bar was set. It always seemed astronomically high . . . until it became just out of my grasp.

Sadly, *Newsweek* magazine went out of print on January 1, 2013. Odd as it may sound, I'll always be indebted to an out-of-print magazine for helping me become the person I am today.

REVIEW

Yehong's strongest skill here is her powerful language and poetic use of metaphors. One of the highlights of the essay is her description of how reading *Newsweek* humbled her, remarking that she was used to feeling "gifted" but now felt like she had been living in the Dark Ages. Her answer of the prompt is spot-on, truly expressing precisely how the experience marked a transition from childhood to adulthood.

Yehong could have elaborated on why being interested in *Newsweek* was such a surprise for her. She also could have chosen a more reflective and thoughtful conclusion to end an otherwise very strong piece of writing. There is definitely an irony between what was at the time an "out-of-print magazine" and her "natural intellectual curiosity" that could have been teased out further.

—Beth Young

III. IDENTITY

Who are you? That's the question the essays in this chapter attempt to answer.

Of course, we are all complex individuals with many interests and experiences, but the applicants in this chapter refuse to get bogged down in trying to exhaustively represent themselves. Rather, they choose to explore a single component of their identities—one that is often surprising or unexpected.

In this chapter, you will read essays that reveal peculiar interests or shocking experiences—all things that shape the writers' outlooks on life. For example, you will read about a student exploring her family history in the context of her own life and a student discussing her love of punk music and countercultural antics.

As you try to understand who you are, think about specific defining moments in your life. Chances are, you'll realize that you have more to write about than you had previously anticipated.

ALLISON CHANG

Hometown: Bronx, New York, USA
High School: Private school, 189 students in graduating class
Ethnicity: Asian
Gender: Female
GPA: 3.95 out of 4.0
SAT: n/a
ACT: 35
SAT Subject Tests Taken: Mathematics Level 2, Biology E/M, Chemistry
Extracurriculars: Editor in chief of 3 publications, theater company vice president, organizer of school play festival, editor/cartoonist for newspaper
Awards: University of Pennsylvania Book Award, AP Scholar, National Merit semifinalist, school-wide critical personal essay awards
Major: Undecided

ESSAY

Editor's Note: Names in this essay have been redacted for privacy.

Once there was a girl who looked within, found divine peace in her soul, and also had great legs. I am not this girl. I am the girl who discovered herself when she became a human sperm cell. But I'm getting ahead of myself.

It was a dark and stormy night, and I was pissed. I was also stooped over a birthday candle, cramming pages of lines for my role in *Rosencrantz and Guildenstern Are Dead*, an existential behind-the-scenes

71

journey of two obscure characters from *Hamlet*. It's an "absurdist tragi-comedy," much like that evening in the midst of Hurricane Sandy.

I had a week off from school to fully embody Rosencrantz. Or Guildenstern? This was half of the problem: "Roz" and "Guil" are so identical that even they forget who they are. Which led to the other half of the problem: D——, my onstage counterpart. Except, he wasn't the issue. I was. See, D—— and I were supposed to be interchangeable, and as a pale male, he looked the part. As an Asian girl, I did not.

I'd often been the only cast member "of color" in shows written for white actors, and I'd taught myself to forget that an audience rarely saw past my alienating physiognomy. But this show was different. During each rehearsal, I asked myself, "Who should I be?" I should be D——, Rosencrantz, or Guildenstern, but certainly not me. My character's basic identity clashed with my own; I wasn't just out of place, I was wrong.

Still, I didn't want anyone's pity, so when D—— offered to run lines, I shut the door on him. Literally. "Are you kidding me? I drove for an hour just to get here!" he said, barely audible through Sandy's howling winds and the sturdy oak of my front door. Nevertheless, in the spirit of October, the month of Columbus Day, I let the white man enter my home. The white man ate all my Triscuits.

I went to the next rehearsal despondent; my study of the white man had left me hungrier and less self-assured than ever. What happened then was destiny. Destiny in the form of a cocoon-like cape and oval-shaped hat, both made of rigid, shiny white vinyl. Our costumes were meant to resemble chess pawns (symbolizing our place in *Hamlet*'s political game), but it didn't matter one bit. The moment I saw that sperm suit, I felt a strange tingling in my gut. At first, I thought it was indigestion, but then I realized: It was true love.

I tried it on, consummating our union. It was very meta. The hat itched and the cape squeaked, but my love knew no bounds. I gazed in the mirror, admiring my transformation into a haploid cell. Then I laughed and laughed.

On average, 280 million human sperm compete to fertilize an egg—odds that put even college admissions to shame. One sperm's life may seem pointless, but en masse, those cells are responsible for all of human evolution. And that's because a sperm doesn't weigh its chances; it dives headfirst into the unknown. To live without fear, to have confidence in my convictions, and to not worry one bit about how others viewed me: I wanted to be like that.

I burst onto center stage. We were pressed for time, but I couldn't hold back; for the first time in a while, I knew exactly who I was. I vigorously spread the good word as my costume gleamed under the spotlights, reflecting my newfound enlightenment. The director gaped, then barked, "What the hell?!"

I was momentarily crushed, but then I remembered: I'm a sperm, and a sperm doesn't quit! To this day, I keep that mantra close to my heart. Here's the moral of the story, the crux of the tale: If you're swimming upstream, and it all seems for naught, don't lose hope, just give it all you've got!

REVIEW

This essay starts off creatively to clearly define Allison's sarcastic, humorous, and honest voice. Allison writes about her ability to persevere through her anecdote of a play and a wonderfully crafted analogy of herself as a sperm. The introduction of this analogy is at first strange, but upon closer examination, it is quite clever; Allison brings the entire essay around to finally hit on the lesson she learned and showcase her personality.

The central idea of her essay tells something about Allison that can be seen nowhere else in the Common Application. She discusses her previous experience of striving forward by detailing her involvement in a play. Her carefully crafted diction and vivid imagery propels this piece forward.

What makes this essay even stronger is Allison's style of writing. She diligently switches between long and short sentences that serve to highlight her point, idea, and situation. There is a perfect balance of detailed description and pithy statements. Ultimately, Allison's essay makes the audience eager to read onward to know her story, thoughts, and aspirations. The essay begins, continues, and ends elegantly and beautifully.

—Ellen Zhang

CATHERINE ZHANG

Hometown: Plano, Texas, USA
High School: Public school, 1,390 students in graduating class
Ethnicity: Asian
Gender: Female
GPA: 4.6 out of 5.0
SAT: Reading 750, Math 800, Writing 760
ACT: n/a
SAT Subject Tests Taken: U.S. History, Mathematics Level 2, Literature, World History
Extracurriculars: Texas Junior State of America Speaker of the House, copresident of the Junior World Affairs Council, columnist for the *Dallas Morning News*, Public Forum Debate Captain of the Plano West Speech and Debate team, and student liaison to the Plano Independent School District Board of Trustees
Awards: National Merit Finalist, Academic WorldQuest Champion, International Public Policy Forum semifinalist, Texas Forensic Association Public Forum Debate quarterfinalist, TEDxPlano Speaker
Major: Government and Economics

ESSAY

Eleventh grade. This is a combat zone.

The American Studies classroom is adorned with shiny gold stars, glimmering like military medallions. They are a powerful reminder of the war cause—the preservation of the American meritocracy, threatened by the authoritarian oppressor on the other side of the pentagonal room. The stars are intended to reward students who put forth effort in class, but I know that Coach Jones, as a skilled expert in proxy wars, hands my nemesis Kierra two rows of the stickers just to spite me.

The edgy situation is reminiscent of preschool, when my Chinese class archrival received two fistfuls of green tea candy for reading the text twelve times, instead of the assigned ten. Deeply enticed by the prospect of a sugar high, I nested myself in the closet and pored over the reading more than 100 times. Thirteen years later, the difference is in the sincerity: jokingly attempting to tussle, Kierra and I are betrayed by our stern faces and collapse into a fit of laughter. The false seriousness of the ordeal adds well-needed levity to our classroom setting.

I am a Russian nesting doll, holding the essence of my former selves—one era in each shell. For one of my early assignments, I channeled the spirit of my kindergarten self—who zealously slayed foreign heads of states in the school play as a U.S. diplomat—and taught my classmates a segment of the American Revolution. Choosing to take an interactive approach, I stood at the front of the classroom as George Washington, commanding my "troops" at Valley Forge to teeter on one foot, simulating fatigue. *If you sit down, you're dead,* I warned. As they grew tired, I instructed them to sit down in chunks. *One group down due to starvation. Another for disease. Another for deserting.* For a long-term assignment, I revived my expressive eighth grade self—who penned every soul-stirring emotion, academic question, or bus-ride philosophy into angst-ridden ballads with ABAB rhyme schemes—and found a creative outlet. Originally intended for approximately 20 assigned writing prompts, my American Studies blog took on a life of its own. Students I had never met sympathized with my college anxieties, laughed along with my struggle to craft my own identity on Twitter, and listened to me recount my experiences— *ridiculous conversations relating every Bob Dylan song to bimetallism, dinner at an old Chinese restaurant, hysterical all-nighters in Boston with the debate team.* In American Studies, the train of my youth barreled down on me with a Doppler effect, growing higher in pitch with a euphoric squeal. My most redeeming characteristics—*inquisitiveness, creativity, candor*—while sometimes lost in the whir of high school, resurged all at once.

This is only possible in a place where I can spontaneously walk laps in the middle of a Great Depression lecture, create unicorn short films relevant to the Roaring Twenties, and analyze Kanye West's latest album as part of class curriculum. During one of my favorite activities, my American Studies classmates and I moved to the verdant lawn of our high school campus and pretended to be transcendentalists, reveling in the silence of our environment. I opened my moleskin journal and let my intuition guide me—painting abstract figures in light washes of color, smearing the patterns with my fingers, dribbling vivid watercolors onto the lined page. American Studies is a class that melds elementary art class with 19th century movements, simplicity with profundity. It is a place that feels like home. Here, the treasured center of my Russian nesting doll carries the essence of my youth outward and simultaneously draws the wisdom and underlying maturity of exterior shells inward to my existing self. My youthful optimism is tempered only by my perspective.

I am at my age, below it, and above it, all at once.

REVIEW

From the first line, Catherine grabs the reader's attention: two short and punctuated sentences that help to draw the reader in. From there, Catherine successfully weaves her story with insight into her character at various points throughout her life, in addition to providing some perspective on the way that she views her education.

Catherine also makes effective use of two extended metaphors throughout this piece—the comparison of eleventh grade to a "combat zone" and the comparison of herself to a Russian nesting doll. These both work well, but working with multiple metaphors simultaneously in such a short piece does run the risk of becoming convoluted. Catherine might have also benefited by getting to the point of the prompt earlier: while the initial exposition is interesting and insightful, it takes a little while before the reader really gets a sense of her personality.

—Brian Yu

YUKI ZBYTOVSKY

Hometown: Hawi, Hawaii, USA
High School: Public school, 67 students in graduating class
Ethnicity: Asian
Gender: Female
GPA: 4.2 out of 4.0
SAT: Reading 660, Math 710, Writing 660
ACT: 32
SAT Subject Tests Taken: n/a
Extracurriculars: Upolu Sediment Mitigation Project coordinator, Kohala Student Credit Union vice president, Kohala Leo's Club (Youth branch of the international Lion's Club) president, varsity cross-country captain, varsity track and field captain
Awards: Kohala Merit Shield recipient, Academic Achievement Awards, Academic Honor Roll Award, Empower Accelerated Reader State Award, class rank 1
Major: Psychology

ESSAY

My story begins even before I was born. My father lived in a world of oppression and persecution. As a child in Czechoslovakia ravaged by Communism, he was compelled to escape to the United States. Later, on the other side of the world, my mother struggled with poverty in Osaka, Japan. How these two distant individuals encountered each other is another marvelous story all on its own. These are the remarkable individuals who created the person I am today. While I am the first generation in my family to be raised in the United States, I still contain a blend of both my parents' cultures.

After I was born in Japan my parents moved to Lake Tahoe, Nevada. Yet that was not our permanent home. Half of the time was spent sailing on the Royal Caribbean Cruise lines on which my father performed. My mother was his assistant, and I was the sweet girl who would be a part of his magic tricks. I also entertained with other performances on the ship. We sailed to a variety of locations including Alaska, the Bahamas, and sometimes to Europe. From a young age, I was exposed to a variety of people every week; socialization became effortless.

The cruise ship would often dock in Cozumel, Mexico, and due to that convenience my family and I moved to the tiny island. At the age of four Mexico became my home. My parents did not hesitate to enroll me in a Spanish school despite my not knowing how to speak the local tongue. My young, flexible mind allowed the new language to easily roll off of my tongue.

All the while, my mother also taught me Japanese. My grandparents who still live in Japan do not speak English and I needed a way to communicate with them. I became a child who spoke Spanish in school, English at home, and Japanese on the phone! For periods of time when my father had lengthier performing tours on the cruise ships, my mother and I would visit my grandparents in Japan. I attended the local school there. My elementary school years were spent floating back and forth between learning calligraphy in Japanese schools and being educated on Independence from Spain in Mexican schools.

How did I end up in Hawaii? I can only seem to recall that the move was because the islands are closer to Japan in order to visit my family. Today, a tiny and secluded community called Hawi is my home. Hawi's main struggle is to provide numerous resources as larger cities in the modern world. Despite this, the tiny town teaches its citizens lessons that are essential for well being and happiness. This population has educated me in the most imperative lessons and principles I carry with me wherever I venture. The Ohana, or "family" lifestyle has made me a community oriented, social individual who enjoys company and companionship. This rural area also emphasizes the value of dependence on one another, supporting one's peers, and the importance of making true connections and friendships.

My background is an essential aspect of who I am today. My parents bring together two vastly different cultures; they educate me with the best aspects of both. Travel has allowed me to have an exposure to a vast array of societies, which in turn, has made me comfortable in many different populations. Tied together with the loving and community-oriented lifestyle Hawaii has taught me, I have matured to become a mixture of different cultures and experiences within the common community of my mind. The result? My passion is in discovery. My advantage is my experience. My distinction is my diversity.

REVIEW

Yuki's essay is among the most personal and most effective I have ever read. She does a fantastic job of weaving together a narrative of her life, telling a story that takes the reader from her birth through the experiences that shaped the person she is today. She starts out by mentioning the vastly different backgrounds of her parents, setting the stage for an essay in which she will discuss the diversity of places in which she has lived.

It is a little bit of a risk to start off a college essay by talking about someone else, because it is important to make sure that your essay is about you. The stereotypical example of this mistake is an essay that expresses undying adulation of a parent. No matter how well written it is, an admission officer might read the essay and wish he could admit the applicant's mother. After reading your essay, admission officers should have another reason to advocate for your application. Yuki's essay certainly succeeds in this regard. Because of her personal story, it would be impossible to discuss how she's lived in Nevada, Mexico, Japan, and Hawaii without mentioning her parents.

In this essay, she provides the reader with a background that gives essential context to the rest of her application. She is successful because she is able to mention her exciting personal background without making the mistake of writing an essay about someone else. Yuki comes across as smart, articulate, and motivated without telling you she's any of those things.

—Ryan O'Meara

MICHAEL LIU

Hometown: Toronto, Canada
High School: Private school, 119 students in graduating class
Ethnicity: Asian
Gender: Male
GPA: 4.0 out of 4.0
SAT: Reading 750, Math 800, Writing 780
ACT: n/a
SAT Subject Tests Taken: Biology E/M, Chemistry, Spanish
Extracurriculars: Research, Brain Bee, newspaper editorship, varsity baseball, and Positive Mental Health
Awards: Canada's Top 20 Under 20, International Brain Bee Honors, Sanofi BioGENEius Research Award, UTS School Pin Award and DECA International Honors
Major: Human Developmental and Regenerative Biology

ESSAY

A loud fart greeted me at the doorway of the ICU suite. Tim, a scrawny child of nine years, was sprawled across the bed, clutching a deflated Whoopee Cushion.

"Excuse you!" he declared, his scolding tone belied by a wide grin.

I threw up my hands apologetically, chuckling. Reaching across the overbed table, I grabbed his chart to update my research notes. Tim had been diagnosed with stage-IV glioblastoma, an aggressive cancer of the brain.

"By the way, I have something for you." I handed Tim the latest copy of *Popular Science*. His eyes lit up instantly, beaming as he flipped to the first page.

His reaction was incredibly touching. Despite a bleak prognosis, his playful antics continued to reflect a *joie de vivre*. The happy-go-lucky joy he embodied was reminiscent of a past that I had mistakenly cast aside.

That night, after entering the final set of data, I fell asleep at the workstation outside Tim's room. The green-padded hospital chair, redolent of the park benches I once slept on, evoked further nostalgia. When my family immigrated to Canada in 2001, our one-room apartment had not yet been vacated. And although we were not well-off, my fondest memories are of my early childhood. My mother and I used to trek through the cherry blossom trees of High Park en-route to daycare. As we would chase each other around and around, ochre branches towered overhead and petals enveloped us like pink raindrops. We lived by the same mantra as Tim: to cherish every moment, raw and unbridled.

Seven years later, my parents' painstaking effort allowed me to receive an extraordinary education at UTS. While preparing for my first research internship, I came across my current role model: Dr. Ben Carson, a neurosurgeon whose remarkable discipline elevated him from humble beginnings. To justify my parents' struggles, I resolved to follow in his footsteps. However, in a race to compete with my exceptional peers, I was blinded by ambition and goals. The curiosity that I once held for learning disappeared, replaced by an infatuation with marks and quantitative validations. On centerfield, I no longer felt the rush and freedom of chasing down a fly ball, consumed instead by the prospect of it meeting the grass.

My experiences in the hospital eventually dispelled this mindset. No matter how intently doctors and nurses persevere against it, death is an unavoidable reality. Patients like Tim are intimately familiar with this inevitability, and so they treasure each second as if it was their last. But do we need to be dying to start appreciating what we have? In the face of limited days, my fears—of judgement, failure, and expectation—become insignificant. If these stubborn clashes with death are ill-fated, then that is all the more reason to enjoy the journey. The connections with patients, each as unique and inspiring as the next, are meaningful remembrances of my time here.

I now celebrate life with a new perspective, enjoying both the periphery and the final destination. My infrequent visits to relatives uptown are becoming monthly cathartic sessions to horrendously belch out karaoke lyrics. My rushed workouts are becoming runs through the natural reserve of the Don Valley. A copy of Borges's *Instantes* lies by my nightstand, a morning reminder to savour the day without restraint or reservation. Recently, I opened up about my body dysmorphia and founded the Positive Mental Health Initiative, in hopes of liberating myself and those also suffering silently in my school.

For me, the hospital is much more than a place of healing. It is my muse, a place where seemingly innocuous exchanges revolutionized my values. It is my salvation, a place that has made palpable the beauty and fragility of life. Above all, it is my sanctuary, a place where my doubts became certainty; my myopia, clarity; and my apathy, excitement. Within these sterile walls, I am most human—alive again.

REVIEW

I have often heard "the key to a good essay is personality." There are few things worse than an essay that reads like a résumé. However, personality needs to be added in a way that is tasteful and subtle. If not, college essays come off like Mad Libs, where the blank spaces call for obscure artists and writers that somehow suggest applicants are fit for college. It is in this effort to strike a perfect balance between genuine and constructed personality that many essays fall apart.

This essay, for the most part, avoids falling into that pit. The author writes about his background in a way that is unique and helps build his persona. But at some moments, the essay sounds a little cliché. For example, the second-to-last paragraph posits that the author's experience with Michael completely turned his life around, and although this might be true, it can be perceived as a try-hard attempt to sound overly profound and enlightened.

In addition, try to avoid worn-out phrases, such as "joie de vivre" or "happy-go-lucky"—those same emotions can be evoked with other interesting words.

One more point to mention: it is important to assume that your reader knows absolutely nothing about you. Avoid using initials, such as UTS (University of Toronto Schools), and make sure to contextualize as much as necessary without drawing away from the central point of your essay.

Still, despite some clichés, this essay does a fantastic job of sharing the author's unique experiences and explaining why those experiences are significant.

—Ignacio Sabate

SOPHIA HIGGINS

Hometown: Bethesda, Maryland, USA
High School: Public school, 450 students in graduating class
Ethnicity: Black, African American
Gender: Female
GPA: 3.94 out of 4.0
SAT: Reading 750, Math 770, Writing 800
ACT: n/a
SAT Subject Tests Taken: Mathematics Level 2, Biology E/M, U.S. History
Extracurriculars: Shakespeare Club president/director, French Club president, literary magazine editor in chief, newspaper creative writing editor, preprofessional musical theater program outside of school
Awards: Second place Poetry Out Loud competition, two honorable mentions in Scholastic Art and Writing awards, AP Scholar with Distinction
Major: Philosophy

ESSAY

"Black Eyeliner Does Not Make You a Non-Conformist"

Several years ago, my mother told me I listen to "white people music." And I suppose that's true—rock 'n' roll tends to spring from the middle-class basements of young, white men. Though I did point out that its origins trace back to jazz musicians of the Harlem Renaissance.

Also that one of the greatest guitarists of all time—dear Mr. Hendrix; may he rest in peace—was black.

My devotion to punk rock began in seventh grade, when Green Day's "Boulevard of Broken Dreams" came up on my iTunes shuffle. I started to look into their other releases, eventually immersing myself into the complete punk discography. My mother, having grown up in a racially segregated New York, was more likely to listen to Stevie Wonder than Stevie Nicks. But, she must have figured, to each her own.

So while my compatriots indulged in the music of Taylor Swift, One Direction, and Lady Gaga, my tacky Hot Topic headphones blasted Green Day, Ramones, and The Clash. My young adolescent ears drank in the raw, chaotic beauty, an echo of the pain of the past. The thrashing, pulsating vitality of the instruments painted a picture, connecting me to the disillusioned kids who launched an epic movement of liberation some 40 years ago.

Punkers question authority. Aggressively contrarian, they advocate for the other side—the side that seemed smothered silent during the post-Vietnam era. They rejected the established norms. They spoke out and weren't afraid.

I had always felt different from my peers. In my girls' prep school, the goal was to be blond and good at soccer. I was neither, which automatically deemed me "uncool." I had a few close friends but never felt like I was part of a whole.

Then came the punk philosophy, for the outliers, for those who were different. That was something I could be part of.

Instead of trying to conform to my peers, I adopted an anti-conformist attitude. Much like the prematurely grey anti-hero of my favorite book, I sneered at all the "phonies" around me. I resented anything popular. Uggs? Wouldn't buy them. Yoga pants? Never. Starbucks? Well, I could make a few concessions.

Identity

But I felt more cynical than liberated. I wasted so much energy on being different that I lost track of what actually made me happy. I insisted I didn't care what people thought of me, which was true. Yet if I based my actions almost solely on their behavior, how could I deny their influence?

Luckily, as I transitioned from a private school to a brand new public high school, I got to clean the slate. I bought yoga pants and found they were comfortable. I listened to a wider variety of music, even the kind that wasn't 100% hardcore punk. And I was happier.

I revised my punk philosophy: Do as you like—whether it fits into the "system" or not.

The Beatles's "Revolution" lyrics sum it up well:

You tell me it's the institution
Well, you know
You'd better free your mind instead

What I think Lennon was getting at is questioning everything does not entail opposing everything. Defiance for the sake of defiance is unproductive at best, destructive at worst.

I believe in life's greater Truths, like Love and Justice. These Truths are what should govern my actions—not what's popular and what isn't. Striving to act on these ideals has helped me stay true to myself, regardless of what's considered "conformist."

Perhaps I've failed the punk movement. We'll have to wait and see.

In the meantime, I'll do what makes me happy and change what doesn't. I'll wear Doc Martens instead of Uggs; I'll partake in a grande pumpkin spice latte; I'll watch Gossip Girl; I'll blare my favorite guitar solo over the speakers in my room.

And that's as punk as it gets.

REVIEW

Sophia's essay—a pitch-perfect portrait of coming-of-age malaise—shows that you don't need some monumental event or life-changing epiphany to craft a compelling narrative. Not much happens over the 647 words of this essay, but the soul is in the details: the nods to her mother, the subtle *Catcher in the Rye* allusion, the levity to be found in her unyielding fondness for lattes.

This essay follows a relatable and adaptable template: let's call it the "blind-but-now-I-see" script. Sophia opens the piece as a causeless rebel (rocking out to Green Day, granted), but blooms into a more nuanced being with a worldview of her own making. Importantly, the young heroine's quest is shown as much as told, with motifs like the yoga pants and Uggs serving as markers of her growing maturity. The essay also showcases Sophia's mastery of cadence—making good use of the em-dash and colon—and her willingness to experiment with prose as she spells out her capital-T Truths. Though Sophia's story has been told and retold between the covers of countless young adult novels, she tells it with wit and warmth, portraying herself to admissions officers as a particularly self-aware, free-thinking applicant.

—Daphne C. Thompson

LEAH MARSH

Hometown: Port Angeles, Washington, USA
High School: Public school, 255 students in graduating class
Ethnicity: White
Gender: Female
GPA: 4.0 out of 4.0
SAT: Reading 760, Math 800, Writing 780
ACT: n/a
SAT Subject Tests Taken: Biology E/M, Spanish
Extracurriculars: Chamber orchestra concertmaster; Key Club
    president; National Honor Society copresident
Awards: National Merit finalist
Major: Molecular and Cellular Biology

ESSAY

My town, being average in most respects, doesn't make it into the
news a lot. But when we do, we do it with gusto: one recent event
that got us on TV was when a man drove a bulldozer through several
neighbors' houses. But notable, perhaps, on a deeper level than the
angry bulldozer rampage is the Elwha River Restoration. In remov-
ing the two-century-old dams on the Elwha River, we have, among
other things, made it possible for the salmon of the Elwha to follow
their ancient instincts and return all the way home.

In some ways, the salmon have been my teachers in this. I have
done my fair share of travel. I love the sense of imminent adventure
at the beginning of a journey, and I love the adventure itself, but

incomparable to both of these is the feeling I get arriving back where I started. It is a sense of sadness that the adventure is over, yes, but also a sense of completion and contentment: I am home. Home not just to my house, but to the Olympic Peninsula, the place I love the most in the world, with its rugged mountains, old-growth rainforests, and rocky beaches.

Perhaps I'm biased. My father is, after all, a ranger at Olympic National Park. But I prefer to think that I am lucky: lucky to live here and lucky to have a dad who has guided me to a true appreciation for the miracles of nature that surround me. Long before I can remember (though pictures will attest), he and my mom would carry me in the baby backpack out on family adventures. Later, I could get through hikes on my own two feet.

Getting my froggy boots muddy was always fun, but some element of the nature around me invariably provided the real wow factor (even once I outgrew the froggy boots): the mighty old-growth evergreens of the Hoh Rainforest, shrouded in their mossy veils; the breaching whale and her baby off of First Beach, on their way to Alaska for the summer; the ethereal beauty of twinkling bioluminescence in Freshwater Bay; or the mountain goat, just a few yards away, staring at me as I rounded a corner on a Hurricane Ridge trail.

Yes, I am undoubtedly lucky to live in such an amazing place. The Olympic Peninsula contains adventures enough for a lifetime. But I thirst for travel; there is an entire world to explore, so why should I stop at one corner of it? Like the salmon, I will make long journeys to faraway lands (or in their case, waters). And even though we don't yet understand the mechanism by which salmon are able to return to the exact spot of their birth, I do know that no matter where life takes me and no matter where I finally settle, the Olympic Peninsula will always be my home.

REVIEW

In this essay, Leah writes about her home, specifically discussing the beauty of where she grew up and her feelings toward her environment. She creatively introduces her sense of home using an incident relating to salmon. Then, Leah uses this incident as an analogy to her deep feeling of home.

Leah's strongest paragraph, the third one, details what home means to her through vivid, sensory detail. The usage of proper nouns such as Hoh Rainforest and First Beach makes this essay more realistic, adding to her nostalgic and awed tone.

Leah ties up this essay by appealing to a broader picture, for although she loves her home, she yearns for more—the more is something college can provide. Simultaneously, she writes that her home is still her home, implying she is sensible and grounded. This essay is well crafted, but it could have been stronger if Leah elaborated on what it means for her home to be home, and how that will change her future plans.

Overall, the essay is wonderfully written through conveying Leah's appreciation for nature and life—things that are not showcased in any other aspect of the Common Application. However, the essay could have been more memorable if Leah detailed how the environment has changed her own beliefs and views leading to her current commitments and future goals. Ultimately, Leah's conversational tone in tandem with her descriptive diction leaves the reader knowing who she is while wondering who she is to become.

—Ellen Zhang

MATIAS FERANDEL

Hometown: Atlanta, Georgia, USA
High School: Private school, 84 students in graduating class
Ethnicity: Hispanic
Gender: Male
GPA: 4.51 out of 4.0 (weighted)
SAT: Reading 800, Math 740, Writing 770
ACT: n/a
SAT Subject Tests Taken: Mathematics Level 2, Spanish
Extracurriculars: Mock Trial captain, Student Council president, varsity soccer
Awards: Salutatorian, Journal Cup, Yale Book Award, Student Athlete Award
Major: Economics

ESSAY

"Right here," says my dad, motioning to a large booth on the right. It's a cold winter morning and we have not eaten yet, but before picking up the menu and even considering food, we both instinctively reach for the white containers at the end of the table holding the sugar packets. He takes eleven blue packets of Equal and I take eleven yellow packets of Splenda. Don't worry; it's not for our coffee.

We lay out the packets of sugar across the table in 4-4-2 formations and begin our postgame discussion tradition. He walks me through his observations as he slides the fictional players across the table: the gaps between the midfield and the forward which did not allow us to move the ball out, the positioning of the outside mid-fielder which developed the first goal, our defensive coordination as the ball was switched across the field, everything.

Countless sugar packets have swept across our tables over the past ten years. However, out of the hundreds of times we have sat down to reflect on the day's events, there is one reoccurring message that has truly stuck in my mind.

"You play well when you hustle."

In the context of soccer, hustle is what dictates my level of satisfaction following a game or practice. I do not dwell over a poor touch, a bad pass or a missed shot because these are instantaneous mistakes. There is little I can change in the moment. However, I am always accountable for my work ethic; this is within my control. And it is only on the nights when I walk off the field with sore legs, lightheaded and a dry throat that I feel satisfied with my performance.

Over time this idea has become one of my life mantras because I apply it to everything I do. In Mock Trial, hustle means reading the case over and over until I can recall the nuances of different case laws and quote them during an objection without second guessing myself. It means knowing the affidavit of my witnesses better than any other person in the courtroom so when I stand up for cross examination I can catch even the slightest deviation in a witness' answer and use his words against him. I cannot feel content with my performance unless I reach this level understanding.

Hustle is essential to me because regardless of the result, it brings out the very best I have to offer. There are no regrets when I hustle.

REVIEW

Matias delves right into the action in this essay. Instead of picking up the menu and flipping through the pancakes and coffees at the restaurant, he and his father begin to arrange sweetener packets. Right away, he has grabbed the audience's attention.

The action begins; he describes how his father moves the sugar packets to model a soccer game. The heart of his essay is the "hustle," which he doesn't mention until about halfway through—Matias could have strengthened his essay by introducing this concept earlier in his essay. But when it finally appears in the body of his essay, there is an instant transformation. Instead of using one sport, one activity, or one event to depict himself, Matias chose to use a concept that he deems essential to his being. What makes him special? Soccer? Maybe. Mock trial? Perhaps. But even more than both of the above, his hustle is what sets him apart from others. Instead of using the lens of his extracurriculars to view himself, Matias uses his character to shed light on his passions and hobbies.

He could certainly have afforded to expand on the topic of this hustle: there seems to be a bit of a rush in the pace when he is explaining what "hustle" means in the context of soccer and mock trial. Overall, this essay is short and sweet; it is succinct and successfully paints a picture of the author—this is crucial.

—Amy Zhao

JENNIFER LI

Hometown: Washington, DC, USA
High School: Public school, 353 students in graduating class
Ethnicity: Asian
Gender: Female
GPA: 4.0 out of 4.0
SAT: n/a
ACT: Prefer not to answer
SAT Subject Tests Taken: Mathematics Level 1, Mathematics Level 2, Chemistry, French, U.S. History, World History
Extracurriculars: Student body president; Student Government Association; teacher and manager, The BUTTERFLY Initiative (a nonprofit organization that teaches elementary school students French); team captain, Harvard Model Congress; Student Ambassador and tour guide; member of varsity swimming and cross-country teams
Awards: DC Public School Seal of Biliteracy in French
Major: Government and Social Studies

ESSAY

In class on the first day of freshman year, I discovered chewed wads of gum stuck underneath my desk. I found half-eaten chicken wings in toilets. The hallways smelled of cigarettes. During lunch, a fight broke out. I tried to get away, but I got shoved against a locker by the crowd. That afternoon, the first alarm was intentionally set off in the boys' bathroom, leading to a flood and evacuation. Welcome to

Woodrow Wilson High School, or, as our principal likes to call it, "the model urban high school in America."

I am a product of DC Public Schools. Although my high school is situated in the predominantly white, upper-middle class neighborhood where I grew up, it draws students from all eight wards in the city, some of which are plagued by poverty. These conditions contrasted with my ideas of what a high school in an upper-middle class ward would be like. There were lessons that I was bound to learn. My first impression of Wilson's disorder is not how I ultimately ended up viewing Wilson.

I was one short student lost in a sea of 1,802 students. It was confusing to be a stranger amongst the waves. There were issues that I wanted to change. I wanted to clean up the sunflower seeds that littered the halls and pick up the hair balls that lined the floors. I also wanted to be the voice for students and make their Wilson experience better. I decided to get involved in our Student Government Association with the hope of improving my school's environment. Over time, I developed an ambitious goal of representing the student body during my senior year. And this June, I was elected to be Student Body President.

It is impossible to know all of Wilson's 1,802 students, but it is possible to represent them. I love when my peers, especially underclassmen who I do not know, approach me when they have a suggestion about how to make Wilson better. I am glad that underclassmen talk to me; hopefully it is because they think I am open to meeting new people. And I get a rush when I stand up on the stage of our auditorium to welcome the students.

I feel lucky to have spent four years in one of the few local high schools where students of different ethnicities, socioeconomic backgrounds, religions, and sexual orientations can coexist. I have learned to treat interactions as valuable lessons rather than awkward conversations. By taking time to know my peers, I have learned about Shy

Glizzy, mumbo sauce, and the art of cornrowing. And more importantly, I have been able to create new friendships and build a cohesive community within our school.

While there is still gum stuck underneath desks, and other imperfections still exist, I have learned to deal with adversity through courage and perseverance. Adversity like me jumping through hoops to organize my school's forum for all six DC mayoral candidates. Adversity like the Westboro Baptist Church actively attacking our homosexual principal, Mr. Cahall, on the basis of his sexual preference. My perseverance to help coordinate a peaceful counter-protest to support Mr. Cahall. Nothing makes me prouder than to be here, embodying all of the voices at Wilson.

If given the chance to study at Harvard, I will remember that every time one human meets another, there is an opportunity to teach—and more importantly, to learn. The wider the gap—be it racial, religious, ideological, economic—the more we have to share with each other. I hope to carry this lesson with me and all those that I've learned at Wilson to the Harvard Undergraduate Council. Although I probably will not find half-eaten chicken wings littering the halls of Harvard, I hope to continue advocating for those around me.

REVIEW

In this essay, Jennifer paints a vivid picture of her role in improving a messy public school. The first paragraph is the strongest, as it concisely uses specific details to capture the reader in Jennifer's own setting. Her strong use of sensory detail throughout the essay proves crucial for making her list of achievements stand out as a real story rather than a résumé.

While impressive, however, this essay lacks intimacy. The essay would have been more effective if Jennifer offered insight into how she developed true connections with students who came from different backgrounds than her and the challenges she faced in improving the school's environment.

However, Jennifer was able to avoid this downfall with her careful attention to detail and humble disclaimers. She is willing to invest in Harvard's community and has experience with socioeconomic and racial diversity. A more nuanced picture would have had the effect of making this strong essay into a powerful one in its ultimate claim to knowing and loving diversity.

—Elizabeth Sun

ANDREW MOTON

Hometown: Stockton, California, USA
High School: Public school, 422 students in graduating class
Ethnicity: Biracial
Gender: Male
GPA: 4.5 out of 4.0
SAT: Reading 800, Math 800, Writing 800
ACT: 33
SAT Subject Tests Taken: Mathematics Level 2, Biology E/M, Physics, U.S. History
Extracurriculars: Science Bowl team captain, intern at U.S. Congressman Jerry McNerney's District Office, varsity tennis, Interact Club president, senior class president
Awards: Ron Brown Goldman Sachs Scholar; Rotary International Paul Harris Fellow, California Scholarship Federation Sealbearer, National Achievement Scholar; CA Science Olympiad State gold medalist
Major: Environmental Science and Public Policy

ESSAY

For the longest time there were two people waking up in my bed each morning, and neither one of them knew who I was. One boy dedicated his time to observe the remains of an assassin bug, a hugely impactful predator with a name fit for its voracious nature. The other boy spent his early mornings reading the newspaper. A devastating cyclone had just hit the people of Burma, a thuggish ruling junta was causing havoc in their lives, and the young boy had to know about it. Although the two boys didn't fully understand the implications of a loss of a particular species in a food web or restrictive trade policies on poor countries without much arable land, they still yearned for more knowledge.

Who was I? A future lab scientist, or the next president to come out of the state of California? Early on, my mother could see this dichotomy developing within my own personality. I got many puzzled looks when I asked for a subscription to *TIME* magazine along with a microscope kit for my tenth birthday. My career ambitions would seesaw between an astronaut and world traveler. The two Andrews would battle for a supermajority of the hours in each day until I decided to be the critical vote to swing toward one Andrew or the other. These halves behaved like two brothers; a modern day Cain and Abel with my punishment seemingly being eternal self-damnation.

Approaching adolescence, the two Andrews would fight for relevance in my mind. One, an active soccer defender, would yell war cries in the middle of his match in a not-so-well-thought-out attempt at intimidation. The other knew his way around a World Book encyclopedia set, even at the expense of social crucifixion. Stevie Wonder was blasting from speakers as I studied the origins of Greek Democracy. Hardly anyone my age paid attention to news that didn't make headlines. I'd be their CNN, a young Wolf Blitzer, analyzing a multifaceted humanitarian crisis although with little knowledge of historical context. I struggled immensely with the thought of my future. The conclusion drawn from those explanations was simple: the two Andrews had no place together.

After several years of intense self-reflection, I realized college would be the platform where I could passionately grow and find out who I want to be in this world. I could go to an amazing school that has some of the world's best professors and challenging courses that

Identity

push me to consider every side of a complex issue. I can picture myself starting the day studying the decay patterns of radioactive elements and finishing the day by debating the success of the Nuclear Non-Proliferation treaty. Whether I end up working for a private energy corporation or the U.S. State Department, I know at this very moment that this is what I needed all along. I needed an avenue to continue to grow in both of my fields of interest. I would not be limited to one half of my heart. My two Andrews, it turns out, were not mutually exclusive, but rather dependent on one another.

REVIEW

Andrew begins this essay with an engaging paragraph describing two unknown people who shared a bed with him for many years. While grabbing the attention of the reader with an intriguing description of his morning awakenings, Andrew begins to describe the two halves of his intellectual curiosities that shape his ambitions for the future and provide a framework for the remainder of his essay. The meaning of the two mysterious figures becomes clear as Andrew describes the tension between his various passions and how each one has shaped his aspirations.

The strength of Andrew's essay lies in its ability to communicate personal details about his past in an engaging and concise manner. Andrew plays with the dichotomy between the two characters in his bed to reveal a level of personal depth which otherwise falls unnoticed in his application. As he outlines his aspirations for the future we learn more about how he spends his time today. This essay shows us the open mind of an ambitious applicant whose future is still an open book.

—Matias Ferandel

ANDIE TURNER

Hometown: Colorado Springs, Colorado, USA
High School: Public school, 250 students in graduating class
Ethnicity: White
Gender: Female
GPA: 3.98 out of 4.0
SAT: Reading 780, Math 760, Writing 800
ACT: 34
SAT Subject Tests Taken: Mathematics Level 2, Biology E/M, Literature, U.S. History
Extracurriculars: Paint the Town paint instructor, varsity swim and dive team captain, Peer AP Exam Review (PAPER) founder, Women Interested in Science and Engineering (WISE) president, District Gifted-Talented Program peer advisor
Awards: All-American Swimmer, National Merit Scholar finalist, won national publication in *Celebrating Art* Anthology, Lewis Palmer Student of the Year, Ian Weikel Champion of Service award winner
Major: Neurobiology

ESSAY

It was five o'clock in the morning, and an intruder was in my home. His vile gurgling sounds had crawled into my room and slinked under my covers, and his deafening beeps had yanked me from sleep. I now lay frozen, listening intently for any other noises—footsteps, perhaps? The screams of my family members?—but the house fell silent.

Slowly, I slid out of bed and tiptoed into the dark hallway. The intruder was definitely near—his distinct, woody odor had infiltrated the air. And with each timid step toward the kitchen, this scent grew ever thicker until, upon reaching the door, I could hardly breathe. Ever so slowly, I pushed it opened and scanned the room. There, gloating next to the fridge, sat "Mr. Coffee."

Twenty-four hours earlier, this machine was not here. Twenty-four hours earlier, I had risen gently from my sleep and ambled into the kitchen to brew a cup of joe not from a coffeemaker, but from my family's old French press. It was a routine that jump-started every morning: grinding the oh-so-slightly toasted beans into an aromatic dust, blanketing the bottom of the glass vessel, listening to the kettle whistle on the stove, and then submerging the roast to create a bold espresso. After I filled a steaming mug, I'd be energized for the day— infused with caffeine and enthused with the artistic process.

But the press was now missing; its home invaded by this new contraption. Just as my eyes narrowed with suspicion, my yawning father meandered into the room.

"Hey . . . what is this?" I gestured to Mr. Coffee.

"Ah, yes!" he chimed, "That's our new coffeemaker!"

"Oh."

My feeling of betrayal must have been palpable, because he raised his eyebrows sharply. "Is something wrong? Andie, come on—this is much more convenient than the old press."

The machine agreed with him; blinking its bright lights and humming haughtily. Then, as if to prove that it was indeed the most efficient appliance ever created, it once again began to pump out an endless flood of muddy liquid.

I deliberated. My father was right, of course—the French press was unarguably time consuming and cumbersome, especially at 5:00 AM—but it was tangible. It was real. Crafting coffee in the morning afforded me a sense of pride and artistry that always inspired the rest of my day. Every cup was a learning experience—fixing the flavors, tweaking the temperatures—but it was only now, after the press had been replaced, that I realized how much I truly appreciated it.

Our French Press is now long gone, but its memory is a constant reminder to apply meaningful effort and a creative touch to all my endeavours. Whether doing research, coaching a swim practice, or simply playing Scrabble with my family, I invest myself completely. Yes, I may work a little slower, I might go over the top sometimes. But I just don't want to live in a world where the familiar and cherished act of making coffee is replaced by the perfunctory push of a button.

REVIEW

The introduction of Andie's essay sets the stage for what promises to be a frightening account of a home invasion. In the opening paragraph, Andie has effectively conveyed a sense of fear without directly using words such as *scared* or *frightened*. She immerses the audience in a story by using sensory descriptions allowing them to fully engage with the narrative and imagine details for themselves.

Through the story of a coffee machine we learn of Andie's appreciation for fine details and methodical thinking process. The replacement of her French press with an automatic coffee machine is as scary to her as a home invasion because it represents the loss of an artistic practice which is an intrinsic part of her morning routine. More broadly, it can be taken to mean the loss of culture or craftsmanship as she generalizes this example to the rest of the world. Andie's appreciation of something so ordinary demonstrates a level of personal depth which cannot come across on a résumé.

—Matias Ferandel

ERIK FLIEGAUF

Hometown: Hopkinton, Massachusetts, USA
High School: Public school, 295 students in graduating class
Ethnicity: White
Gender: Male
GPA: 4.0 out of 4.0
SAT: Reading 800, Math 750, Writing 760
ACT: n/a
SAT Subject Tests Taken: U.S. History, Mathematics Level 2, and Biology M
Extracurriculars: Drama Club member, National Honor Society president, Students Taking on Poverty president, Men's Chorus member, UNITE Mentoring mentor
Awards: Princeton Book Award, National Merit finalist, Daughters of the American Revolution Good Citizen Award, Salutatorian, AP Scholar with Distinction
Major: Sociology

ESSAY

I didn't see many rainbows in India. They hide in the monsoon rains, or are too frightened by the hot, stifling climate. Likewise, I was terrified of showing that side of myself in a homophobic country, especially to the host family I had grown to love.

"Why India?" my friends would ask. They knew the cruel, anti-gay laws in that country. I knew I had to go anyway. I felt an obligation to see what life must be like when society ignores you, constricts you like a tightly-wound sari. And subconsciously, I hoped that I might somehow change opinions. Yet when I arrived, I was scared to broach the subject, even with Tanmay, my 13-year-old smart but immature, host brother.

Only a pink, flimsy curtain separated our shared bedroom from the corridor, but nevertheless a sort of secret camaraderie developed during our nightly hushed conversation. We hoped Aji and Baba wouldn't hear us. As Tanmay asked me which of the girls on my program I liked, I remembered the sleepovers of my childhood, during which the discussion of romance was dreaded and confusing. Now, I countered with ease. "Sophia is pretty," I diplomatically replied, releasing the moment's tension that only I perceived. I began to enjoy responding to his provocative questions, the answers to which he already knew, teaching him what were accepted topics of discussion within my culture. "What is dating?" "How are babies made?" I reveled in his squirming and shock when I gave a blunt, sex-ed-type answer. "Have you ever liked a girl?" Personal pronouns had never before been so treacherous, nor so masterfully avoided.

I found myself relishing the satisfaction of self-knowledge, the thrill of carrying a secret, the transition from a very private introvert to now a big brother for the second time in my life—candid about everything—except for one.

"He's the biggest homosexual in my class," he snorted, while discussing his classmates. I seized up, but I willed myself to speak, venturing into unsafe airspace.

"Tanmay, you shouldn't make fun of gay people." I sounded like a cheesy tolerance advertisement. "Did you know that they" (the safety of third-person!) "don't choose to be gay?" He disagreed. We continued bantering in the first truly meaningful debate of my life, though the culture clash was played with blunted weapons. The notion of me having gay friends astounded him. The thought of telling him the truth, which for my own safety I couldn't do, was appealing. Instead,

Identity

I took a different risk as I exposed myself to the likelihood of disappointment. "Did you know that in some parts of America, two men or two women can get married?" He did. "What do you think about that?"

I expected him to disapprove and prepared to brush off the ignorance. His experience was far different than my own. I remembered how lucky I was to live in colorful Massachusetts.

After a long pause, he replied. "I think it's good. As long as a gay person doesn't have to marry a non-gay person."

I remember being overwhelmed by the hope that must have spilled from our humid apartment into the street below. I believed then, as now, that I had done a tiny part in the global quest for justice, and I was proud. Or perhaps progress was to come without my actions. Yet the unexpectedness of his affirmation, coupled with the innocent humor of its qualification, made me smile as the night's tropical rains descended on India. We would find out the morning's weather soon enough.

REVIEW

Erik takes a risk in this essay, but he executes it quite effectively. He writes about two topics often recommended to approach with caution in a college essay: traveling abroad and coming out.

However, Erik puts a unique spin on these topics. He narrows in on one specific anecdote of his travel experience, with the location being critical to the worldly nature of the story and his understanding of cultural differences. Similarly, instead of talking solely about his coming out experience, Erik uses this significant aspect of his identity as a way of contextualizing his experiences in a different culture. His story is one about standing firm in his identity and changing a mindset of a young adult. That is where this essay truly shines.

These two topics work together seamlessly to tell a specific story that has shaped his future desires. However, one aspect Erik could have improved upon is letting the story do the telling at the end, as he does through most of his essay. For example, using phrases like "quest for world justice" can be seen as not only cliché but also as a sweeping statement and unrealistic goal.

Erik successfully started with a broad introduction at the beginning, zoomed into a certain anecdote, and zoomed back out at the end. With his captivating language and attention to detail, he successfully engages the reader while taking risks with his essay—risks that worked together to accomplish an effective essay.

—Annie Schugart

SARA FRIEDMAN

Hometown: Sleepy Hollow, New York, USA
High School: Public school, 240 students in graduating class
Ethnicity: White
Gender: Female
GPA: 4.0 out of 4.0
SAT: Reading 760, Math 800, Writing 790
ACT: n/a
SAT Subject Tests Taken: U.S. History, Biology E/M, Literature
Extracurriculars: Orchestra, chorus
Awards: National Merit, Sons of Italy Scholarship, Salutatorian
Major: Biomedical Engineering

ESSAY

Around 2005, my house was constantly strewn with Polly Pockets and Legos. My sister and I liked Polly Pockets, my brother liked Legos, and the amount of time we all channeled into our respective activities was astronomical. We spent more time defining rules of conduct for our Lego world and creating backstories for our Polly Pocket families than we did in the real world. We contemplated the merits of Kraft Mac n' Cheese and focused our entire beings on who would win family game night. We played until we had to go to sleep, and before bedtime, we would say "save the game," and our progress in our imaginary worlds would be waiting for us the next day. The Era of Polly Pockets and Legos was also an era of hopes and dreams, of vivid optimism, of dimples and craft projects and of anything is possible.

The 2005 versions of my siblings and myself were naïve and blissful, with thoughts full of "Honey you have such potential" that were only broken by the occasional bad dreams of things far, far away and impossible. Grown-ups fixed the few problems we had, dealing with an outside world of other grown-ups. We were quick to believe in ourselves, blind to anything that did not smack of positivity. The world of fantasy we three children lived in was heavenly, but soon the Polly Pockets and Legos decorating our house turned into "I'm too old for this" and mounting homework and tangible plans for a future that is no longer a vague dream but a quickly approaching reality.

There is a picture hanging on my wall of me, in 2005, grinning, with lopsided pigtails and a missing tooth. The young me wears the expression of a quintessential child and embodies what my childhood was. My cute 2005 image, unceremoniously hung on the wall to fill a frame, has seen me slowly but surely become distant, changed, grown-up and living in the real world. The girl in the picture does not know that Abraham Lincoln did not valiantly fight to free the slaves out of the goodness of his heart. She does not understand how hard her parents work to have her smiling and carefree, does not know the specifics of sacrifice, delayed gratification, or compromise.

It is hard to say whether 2005 me, full of grand expectations and devoid of realistic notions, would be proud of all I have come to achieve. Surely the image of her hanging for all these years has seen me after I failed a test for the first time, after I published a book, after I "broke up" with my oldest friend, after an article I wrote got translated into Dutch, and after I found out I was first in my class. Hopefully she can forgive me for abandoning my dream to be a movie star and marry a prince. She might not like the person I've become, or she might see herself echoed in me. Maybe she knows for certain when I stopped being a child and replaced my Polly Pockets with homework and plans, but I think it was when I saw her as a person separate from the person I am now.

REVIEW

In this essay, Sara fluidly depicts the changes her personality underwent during her childhood and describes her transition into adulthood. The reader learns a great deal of her past: her innate creativity from experimentation with Polly Pockets, her ability to compromise and work with others, her vitality, positive energy, and appreciation for what her elders have enabled her to achieve. We also learn about her current impressive attributes such as her tenacity, dedication to hard work, and, rather tactfully incorporated without sounding conceited, the fact that she's written a book! The essay beams with maturity, and this tone is maintained consistently. The contemplative opening paragraph shows that Sara puts thought into her reflections and clearly has powerful analytical skills. This is an essential component to any essay—showing that as a talented individual one still has the ability to reflect on one's own development in a critical but fair manner.

The structure of this essay is particularly moving and offers some key takeaways. Sara wisely opens each paragraph with some temporal reference to a distant "then," i.e., 2005, and contrasts this person with whom she is now. Furthermore, the flow of the essay is impactful as it takes the reader on a journey through Sara's mind. In just a few hundred words, we see her pragmatism battling with her hopeless optimism and how she deals with a fairly basic aspect of growing up. The order in which she tells her stories shows the shift she faces as a child who has everything solved by an adult, to becoming the adult who has to solve problems herself. The action-oriented personality she assumes is impressive, and Sara presents herself as someone who is ready to take on the countless challenges that college life will pose.

While very strong, this essay would have been improved with a more clear conclusion. The series of uncertain clauses marked by "might" and "maybe" lead to a less concrete idea of precisely whether Sara has come to terms with her transformation. A clearer final sentence with some more direct analysis would have elevated this piece further.

—Kabir K. Gandhi

IV. OVERCOMING OBSTACLES

Most everyone has faced some adversity in their pre-college life, whether modest, like getting cut during auditions for the school play, or severe, such as being diagnosed with a life-threatening illness. Recounting a story about how you overcame an obstacle or failure is a common essay topic, and it can be compelling regardless of the severity of the obstacle. All of the successful essays in this group, though, go beyond explaining simply how the writer overcame an obstacle and reflect on how that experience has shaped them as a person.

The students in this chapter describe a time they experienced hardship or failure—sometimes a painful process. Each applicant tells the story of his or her own hardships with a sense of thoughtful introspection and authenticity. One student describes coping with the death of a parent, while another recounts her struggle to overcome an eating disorder.

This essay is your chance to show your readers how you've made it through a trying time in your life—one through which you have undoubtedly grown and matured. Use individual anecdotes and striking nuances to let your personal transformation shine to wow admissions officers.

MAUREEN TANG

Hometown: Chino, California, USA
High School: Public school, 698 students in graduating class
Ethnicity: Asian
Gender: Female
GPA: 3.9 out of 4.0
SAT: Reading 680, Math 740, Writing 750
ACT: n/a
SAT Subject Tests Taken: Mathematics Level 2, Biology E/M
Extracurriculars: Varsity Dance Team captain, Associated Student Body Commissioner of Bulletin, Commissioner of Link Crew, teacher and choreographer at Dellos Dance Studios, founder and vice president of Future Business Leaders of America, vice president and activities director of Leo Club
Awards: San Bernardino County Top 1% Junior, 2016 Senior Miss Dance at Legacy Dance Championship Regionals, 2015 National Champion at Revolution Talent Competition, 2015 National Champion at Starbound Dance Competition, Ultimate Husky Finalist
Major: Undecided

ESSAY

As the lively thoughts in my mind battled for priority of investigation, I was more than content sitting in an empty room with bland, white walls and a shabby, old mattress. Contemplating the endless entities of the vast world that I could explore in my third-grade science project made me feel the significance of my imagination in my seemingly insignificant world of a tiny bedroom. Being confined in such a small space never confined me or my thoughts. In fact, the limited resources that I had instigated the limitless ideas and ambitions that filled my mind. Despite the ironically droning sound of silence that seemed to pulsate for hours while the loneliness encapsulated me, my bustling mind kept me occupied. Deeply intrigued, I sat in my room for hours with piles of books without any sense of time because reading was my only source of entertainment. Simply reading about different intellectual topics left me fascinated and aching for more, providing me with an escape from harsh realities. As the hours went by and my bedroom gradually grew dark, I began to hear the twisted symphony of cacophony that occurred routinely every night. My fascinated state-of-mind, however, had grown accustomed to muffling out the terrifying sounds of the breaking dishes, slamming of doors, and forceful shouting. When I heard the sudden slamming of my door, my mother stood at the threshold with a distressed, terrified look on her face. I tried to take a deep breath but my lungs were shaky. Instead of catching the usual whiff of cigarette smoke, I caught an artificially fruity scent that came from a vape. A vape that represented to me more than an e-cigarette that delinquent teenagers brag about owning. A vape that gave me hope. A vape that convinced me it was possible for daddy to stop hitting mommy and to see mommy smile again. A vape that told me not to give up when my dad would come home late from gambling every night. A vape that did not leave me devastated when my father continued to intoxicate himself. A vape that hung onto every last bit of hope even when the stranger I had a difficult time perceiving as "my dad" was thousands of miles away.

My father's departure left my family in a difficult situation, financially and emotionally. From sleeping on the floor of my cousin's house one night to sleeping in a strange motel another, growing up in a constantly changing environment made me thankful to have education as one of the only constants in my life. Although my family was never wealthy, I never felt "poor"; I always felt rich with the extravagance that knowledge provided me with.

Although I often did not sleep in the same bed every night, my dance studio became my second home where I searched for solace. Dance created a liberating atmosphere that left me empowered to conquer any challenge in my life. When the commotions of school and the stresses at home became overwhelming, I could always depend on the simplicity of dance (just music and motion)—yet the art still became so intricately compelling with its freedom of expression and endless possibilities. Despite the athleticism of dance, this artistic outlet gave me a chance to free my mind and to use movement as a reminder that every precious moment of life is one to be celebrated and made the most of.

The world I come from taught me to stop and smell the flowers or, in my case, the vape. Though I was often occupied with worrying about not having the standard resources to succeed, I learned to utilize simplicity to appreciate what I did have. I found inspiration in unconventional objects, scents, and sounds. I instilled the mentality that every problem was merely an illusion of the mind while happiness would come naturally when I made the most of every situation.

REVIEW

In this essay, Maureen shares personal details concerning her family history and explains how they have shaped various aspects of her life beyond home. The inclusion of sensitive details regarding her experiences in a lower socioeconomic class and difficult relationship with her father earn a degree of personal trust from the reader from the outset of her essay. Furthermore, this story demonstrates Maureen's resilient character and willingness to share personal experiences with others.

Through her past, Maureen attempts to explain her current appreciation of education as a means of escape from the harsh realities she faces at home. As described within her essay, a thirst for knowledge and sheer intellectual curiosity allow her to muffle unpleasant disputes between her parents and distance herself mentally from a difficult situation.

Maureen's descriptions of her personal life place her accomplishments within a unique context which, without this essay, may be unappreciated in her application. In doing so, Maureen effectively uses the essay portion of her application to portray her story and her life within a framework which is likely different from most applicants.

—Matias Ferandel

ANGELA HUI

Hometown: San Francisco, California, USA
High School: Private school, 96 students in graduating class
Ethnicity: Asian
Gender: Female
GPA: 4.0 out of 4.0
SAT: Reading 800, Math 780, Writing 800
ACT: n/a
SAT Subject Tests Taken: Mathematics Level 2, Literature, U.S. History
Extracurriculars: President of Asian Club and Chinese Club; Youth Ambassador for Youth Voices on China video competition; ran mental health advocacy blog with over 25k followers; wrote articles for Proud2Bme, an online community in partnership with the National Eating Disorders Association; led community service project encouraging healthy habits in low-income neighborhoods
Awards: AP Scholar with Distinction; National Merit Scholarship recipient; Biology Department Prize; Webster Prize for Outstanding Work in History and Social Science; Certificate of Recognition from California State Assembly
Major: Undecided

ESSAY

Since childhood, I have wanted to know the why and how of everything. I always needed to find the answers to my questions, even if my quest for knowledge meant staring into a black hole of library stacks, *Scientific American* paywalls, and endless Wikipedia articles. Simultaneously overwhelmed and elated by the vastness of the universe, I thought to myself that to live for a thousand years would not be enough; I wanted to see everything, to understand every atom and galaxy and thought in existence.

I was never afraid to look a fungus in the face, to go spelunking through the caverns of calculus and colonialism, so when it came to discovering myself, I was just as willing to trek through uncharted and at times uncomfortable territory.

During the first two years of high school, my facade of overachievement hid a secret spiral into an eating disorder. By the end of tenth grade, I had two Abbot Academy grants, a history department prize, and a medical leave of absence from Andover. Conscious of the stigma surrounding mental illness, I cited "family issues" when my friends, teachers, and acquaintances inquired into the reason for my involuntary homecoming.

Eating disorders are difficult to treat because the afflicted do not want to be treated. But being sent home was exactly the catalyst I needed to recognize the necessity of recovery. I wanted to be able to think again instead of having my head clouded by starvation. I wanted to live a full and meaningful life. So I dutifully swallowed my medication every morning, waiting for my restored neurochemical balance to quell my quieting but continual urges to shrink myself.

Yet even as my mood and temperament improved, it was not enough. To heal fully, I had to dig deeper. I researched eating disorders and mental health extensively, reading everything from *Gaining: The Truth About Life After Eating Disorders* to Dr. Irvin Yalom's *Love's Executioner*, a collection of case studies on existential psychotherapy. From them, I learned to understand the psychological aspects of my condition and to restore order not just in my brain but in my mind. I came to accept that physical growth did not equate to failure, that gaining weight actually meant gaining life. As I abandoned my bad habits, the neural pathways driving my insecurity and compulsions to lose weight finally atrophied.

By the miracles of neuroplasticity and psychological healing, I began to live again. One day I realized that between movie marathons and all-night conversations, picnics in the park and four-hour physics worksheets, I had forgotten the calories in one hundred grams of egg whites, the carbs in an apple, the guilt I once tasted with every morsel of food that slipped past my lips. My cerebral approach to recovery had worked; it was not detached or distant, and by attacking my problem directly, I could solve it.

Overcoming my eating disorder was the greatest challenge of my life. Today I no longer live in fear of food and fat. My recovery inspired me to write publicly about my experiences and to support others through their own difficulties. I only regret wasting so many months suffering in isolation instead of seeking treatment. We must stop viewing mental illness as a secret shame, lest millions of people continue to avoid facing their problems and resign themselves to a life of silent torment.

Until we lift the veil from the darkest parts of the universe, we will never be able to shed light upon them. To live blindly is to live powerlessly. I want to learn as much as I can about the world around me, to seek truth at every juncture, to live the questions and pursue the answers.

REVIEW

Angela has written a brave essay about a personal struggle with an eating disorder. She does a good job introducing her story in a way that feels natural, weaving in her personal struggles with her desire to achieve outwardly successful. The beginning of her story will sound familiar to anyone who has spent time around Harvard students: Angela's curiosity is common among many Harvard students. This essay is successful because she is able to pivot away from what makes her similar and toward what makes her unique.

As she begins to share the details of her struggles with the reader, her writing is effective because the themes she introduced at the beginning of the essay continue to shape how she writes about her struggle with an eating disorder. Detailing how her extensive reading and research led her to move past her eating disorder is powerful. It also shows the reader that the intellectual excitement she displays at the beginning of the essay isn't just for show. When faced with a big struggle, Angela turns back to the intellectual curiosity she described in her introduction. This consistency is noticeable in this tightly-written essay that effectively shows the writer's transformation in the face of difficult circumstances. Angela has taken the greatest challenge of her life and turned it into an effective college essay.

—Ryan O'Meara

CAHLEB DERRY

Hometown: Rockland County, New York, USA
High School: Private boarding school, 170 students in graduating class
Ethnicity: Black, African American
Gender: Male
GPA: 9.51 out of 12.0
SAT: n/a
ACT: 30
SAT Subject Tests Taken: Mathematics Level 1, Biology E/M, French, Literature
Extracurriculars: Cohead of the all-male a capella group the Hotchkiss Bluenotes, captain of the varsity track and field team, class president, member of Disciplinary Committee, proctor in the dormitory, peer counselor for rising sophomores, president of the Black and Hispanic Student Association
Awards: The Wycoff Award for outstanding character, captainship and contribution to the track and field team, All Founders League award for outstanding spirit and contribution to the track and field team, 6th in the triple jump in the New England Class-A D1 Championship (2014), 2nd in the triple jump in the New England Class-A D1 Championship (2015), 1st and being crowned New England Class-A D1 Champion in the Triple Jump (2016)
Major: Undecided

ESSAY

Two hundred and two Hot Wheels cars, each two by five inches long, adorned with flames and spoilers, lined the edges of my room. My mother would urge me to put them away and go play outside, but I never wanted to. I drove those cars all around the house. They intrigued my six-year-old self. I loved my collection that I had hand picked on my own. Every single one of those 99-cent cars was *mine*. I never fathomed, however, that it would not take nearly as long for that collection to disappear as it took to grow. After July 6, 2006, I never saw my collection again.

On that day, I squinted to get one last glance at the front door of my home. 50 Greenridge Way was a quaint, two-story home in a quiet suburb of Rockland County, New York. My mother was six months pregnant with me when my parents signed the papers in 1997. They were proud of themselves—they had something that was theirs. My mother and father were determined to achieve the American Dream. They saved up for their baby grand piano, and they worked hard so that my sister and I could paint our rooms pink and blue like the ones on the cover of PB Teen. They did not know, however, how fast what they attained could disappear. The unanticipated vicissitudes of owning a small business left my parents struggling to pay the mortgage, unable to feed the rapid growth of their dream. They desperately reached out for help and fell victim to a mortgage scam. Legally outsmarted and outspent, my family continued to struggle until we could no longer fight. After thousands of dollars of debt, countless phone calls, and many tears, we lost the battle. On July 6, 2006, we were told we had six hours to get out.

Six hours. *Six* hours to get out of something filled with *nine* years of work, a lot of money and an immeasurable amount of emotion—six hours to pack up our lives and move them somewhere else. Day laborers were instructed to come and throw our belongings onto the front lawn. Family and neighbors flocked over, all agreeing to store as much as they could. I scrambled to find the things important to me. I threw my blankie, my Gameboy and my Build-A-Bear into a small duffle bag. As I rushed into my aunt's car, my eyes glued to the movers tossing my mom's favorite Diego Rivera painting onto the street, I felt uneasy. Many questions should have been going through my eight-year-old head, but only one did: where are my 202 cars?

For the next five years, my family was homeless. Many doors were slammed in our faces, and we were given the "one night maximum" package in many of our family members' homes. However, the takeaway from this experience is not what I learned about the behavior of others—it is what I learned about character. The values that cannot be touched—my experience, resilience, and faith—built more character in me than any two by five inch car or baby grand piano ever will. Losing every single one of our belongings by theft and storage unit auctions, including my 202 cars, showed my family that the intangible things that got us through hardship are everlasting. The six hours spent leaving our home felt so remarkably unequivalent to the nine years we spent enriching it, or the 8 years I spent growing my car collection. However, those unexpected losses taught me that a loss of my possessions was not a loss of my character. Even in the hotels, cars, and basements, this experience showed me that no matter how little my family had, we would always have the privilege to hope.

My family has been pushed into brief bouts of homelessness since the incident, and may be facing our next bout in the coming days. Although I still worry about our financial status, a feeling of overwhelming faith creeps up my spine and deadens that anxiety. Our faith and tenacity will never be plundered like our possessions. My seemingly unshakable phobia of losing "everything" again has diminished over the years because if I lose my possessions again, I know I will not be losing "everything." The next chapter of my life will signal the beginning of newer, and perhaps tougher, challenges, but through all of the uncertainty and worry, I will be letting out a sigh of relief. None of our possessions, including that carefully constructed collection of two hundred and two cars, adorned with flames and spoilers, were the vehicles that drove my family through five years of turmoil. *It was our intangibles that did.*

REVIEW

Homelessness is an incredibly powerful topic to write about. Cahleb approaches the subject with touching candor, detailing how his family lost their home in pursuit of the American Dream, and how he lost his beloved Hot Wheels collection.

But what makes this essay truly remarkable is not the topic; it's the build up. Cahleb begins with the descriptive imagery of his Hot Wheels and uses those cars as a motif throughout the essay. This essay could have easily opened with a line about how he is homeless, but it truly builds up to the moment he realized his family was being kicked out of their home. We feel empathy for this family, and we feel deeply connected to the writer, because we are brought along for the ride.

The strongest aspect of this essay is its seamless incorporation of the 202 Hot Wheels into the overall message of the essay. That message can come off a bit heavy-handed at times; the essay would have benefitted from more showing and less telling. But it is incredibly sincere, and the point is hammered home by the repeated use of the toy cars. By ending with the same image that opened the essay, the writer brings the story full circle, and the reader is left with a deep understanding of not only his hardship, but how he rose above that hardship.

—Leah S. Yared

NIKOLAS PALADINO

Hometown: Paramus, New Jersey, USA
High School: Private all-male parochial school, 178 students in graduating class
Ethnicity: White/Hispanic
Gender: Male
GPA: 106.26 out of 100 (weighted)
SAT: Reading 730, Math 800, Writing 800
ACT: n/a
SAT Subject Tests Taken: Mathematics Level 2, Chemistry, U.S. History
Extracurriculars: Mock Trial Club captain/attorney, chorus baritone leader, Newspaper Club editor in chief, Student Government Association student body vice president, Immaculate Conception HS Theater Lead Actor
Awards: New Jersey Mock Trial State Championship Award, Excellence in English Award, Bergen Catholic High School Alumni Association Scholarship Award, Most Outstanding Soloist Award at Music in the Parks Competition, George Eastman Young Leaders Award
Major: Undecided

ESSAY

I learned the definition of cancer at the age of fourteen. I was taking my chapter 7 biology test when I came upon the last question, "What is cancer?", to which I answered: "The abnormal, unrestricted growth of cells." After handing in the test, I moved on to chapter 8, oblivious then to how earth-shattering such a disease could be.

I learned the meaning of cancer two years later. A girl named Kiersten came into my family by way of my oldest brother who had fallen in love with her. I distinctly recall her hair catching the sea breeze as she walked with us along the Jersey shore, a blonde wave in my surrounding family's sea of brunette. Physically, she may have been different, but she redefined what family meant to me. She attended my concerts, went to my award ceremonies, and helped me study for tests. Whenever I needed support, she was there. Little did I know that our roles would be reversed, forever changing my outlook on life.

Kiersten was diagnosed with Stage II Hodgkin's lymphoma at the age of 22. Tears and hair fell alike after each of her 20 rounds of chemotherapy as we feared the worst. It was an unbearable tragedy— watching someone so vivacious skirt the line between life and death. Her cancer was later classified as refractory, or resistant to treatment. Frustration and despair flooded my mind as I heard this news. And so I prayed. In what universe did this dynamic make any sense? I prayed to God and to even her cancer itself to just leave her alone. Eventually, Kiersten was able to leave the hospital to stay for six weeks at my home.

My family and I transformed the house into an anti-microbial sanctuary, protecting Kiersten from any outside illness. I watched TV with her, baked cookies for her, and observed her persistence as she regained strength and achieved remission. We beat biology, time, and death, all at the same time, with cookies, TV, and friendship. Yet I was so concerned with helping Kiersten that I had not realized how she helped me during her battle with cancer.

I had been so used to solving my problems intellectually that when it came time to emotionally support someone, I was afraid. I could define cancer, but what do I say to someone with it? There were days where I did not think I could be optimistic in the face of such adversity. But the beauty that resulted from sympathizing as opposed to analyzing and putting aside my own worries and troubles for someone else was an enormous epiphany for me. My problems dissipated into thin air the moment I came home and dropped my books and bags to talk with Kiersten. The more I talked, laughed, smiled, and shared memories with her, the more I began to realize all that she had taught me. She influenced me in the fact that she demonstrated the power of loyalty, companionship, and optimism in the face of desperate, life-threatening situations. She showed me the importance of loving to live and living to love. Most of all, she gave me the insight necessary to fully help others not just with intellect and preparation, but with solidarity and compassion. In this way, I became able to help myself and others with not only my brain, but with my heart. And that, in the words of Robert Frost, "has made all the difference."

REVIEW

The strength of this essay comes from the contrast the author sets up in the first two paragraphs. Starting with "I learned the definition of cancer" and then concluding with "I learned the meaning of cancer" establishes that the author is capable of a neat form of introspection that is often ignored: understanding the difference between a word's linguistic function and its various connotations.

From there, the author takes the reader on a tale about a completely different individual—his brother's girlfriend. At first, this is somewhat of a jarring shift, especially considering the specific imagery the author conjures, phrases that often signal an infatuation rather than a platonic relationship. But his tale of Kiersten's battle with cancer makes the reader realize that his relationship is a testament to his ability to sympathize deeply with someone not necessarily confined in the traditional scope of "a family." That alone is a poignant vignette into the author's life, but he drives the point home in the concluding paragraphs by presenting a summary of how the experience impacted his character. The summary itself is notably devoid of platitudes, besides the final two lines. That sort of genuine introspection is endearing to a reader, and presents an almost unfiltered glimpse into the underlying "themes" of his character, which is exactly what an admissions counselor is looking for in an application essay.

The only advice we have for the author: stray away from using so many paired buzz phrases like "intellect and preparation, solidarity and compassion" because it somewhat detracts from the genuineness of the story.

—Brandon J. Dixon

ALLISON RABE

Hometown: Minot, North Dakota, USA
High School: Public school, 449 students in graduating class
Ethnicity: White
Gender: Female
GPA: 4.0 out of 4.0
SAT: n/a
ACT: 35
SAT Subject Tests Taken: Mathematics Level 2, Biology E/M
Extracurriculars: Track and field athlete, volleyball athlete, debate cocaptain, Envirothon participant, National Honor Society participant
Awards: National Merit Scholar, North Dakota Scholar, North Dakota Academic All State Gold Team, runner up state debate, U.S. Representative XI International Junior Forest Contest
Major: Integrative Biology

ESSAY

Family is everything, right? For me, this is especially true. My oldest brother, David, has Asperger's Syndrome. As experts calculated that one out of every 150 babies born in 1995 were born on the Autism spectrum, David had a 0.67 percent chance of having Asperger's. That is, there was a less than one percent chance that he would be excluded and bullied for his eccentricities. There was a less than one percent chance that he would be unable to communicate his extensive knowledge. There was a less than one percent chance that I would have to be a big sister to my older brother. For seventeen years I have lived with and loved my fascinating yet frustrating eldest sibling. I felt sympathy for him, but also admiration. I was amazed by his ability to choose any topic and understand every aspect with tremendous ease. Dinosaurs were his childhood passion and he could identify every skeleton in a museum by the time he was six. While other families traveled to Disneyland, ours visited dinosaur museums. In hopes of absorbing even a small portion of his plethora of information, I stayed at his side on all of his adventures. I looked up at him in awe as he counted the cervical vertebrae of the Apatosaurus and listened intently as he read aloud about the wings of the Archaeopteryx. Together we studied the sediment layers of the Badlands and searched below the KT Boundary for bones. I tagged along, wide-eyed and dreaming of someday becoming as knowledgeable as he was. These experiences ignited my love for science, nature, history, and discovery. As much as I wanted to be like him, this desire was selective. Because of his Asperger's, David had difficulty handling unforeseen circumstances. Many times I was forced to assume control of situations, regardless of my age. Once, on a winter morning many years ago, David and I got into a car accident. The stress was too much for him to handle and he broke down; I was left alone. I took a deep breath, stumbled out of the mangled car, and assumed control of the situation. As I navigated the protocol for car accidents, David remained cemented to his seat, slamming his palms on the steering wheel and bawling uncontrollably. I will never forget the looks of confusion and sympathy I received that day. Experiences similar to this taught me to accept responsibility and remain composed under stress. These situations were not the only time David's inability to conform to societal norms was exposed. During school, he endured bullying and exclusion for his quirks. It was heartbreaking to witness classmates treat him viciously because he was different. It angered me greatly, and I vowed that I would never be a bystander to intolerance. I learned to speak out against injustice and inequality and to stand up for those who could not. Despite my best efforts, some hateful words always slipped past my defense. As a result, my big sister duties did not end in the hallways. At home, many nights were spent defusing the ticking bomb fueled by his bad day. I let his screaming, malicious comments slide off my shoulders. I reciprocated his hate with love and comfort. Weathering these nights taught me to remain peaceful in the face of anger and hostility. Although he may never realize it, my brother permanently and drastically influenced my life in a variety of ways. He encouraged my love of knowledge, ability to assume control, desire to advocate equality, and strength to stay compassionate. Thanks, big brother.

REVIEW

The strength in this essay lies in the different examples and anecdotes Allison shares about her brother. In these specific stories, we can see the ways in which David influenced the writer and shaped her as a person. In the specific anecdotes, we as readers are able to follow along and see how exactly David influenced Allison. The story reaches a pivotal moment when Allison describes the time she and her brother got in a car accident, and she had to step up to solve a problem that her brother was unable to handle. Through this story, Allison demonstrates maturity beyond her years and her ability to handle stress.

Allison's solid narrative storytelling draws the reader in, and her thoughtful and raw descriptions of her brother, in particular, give the reader a vivid image of his personality. The only shortcoming of this essay is that it is written in one big paragraph—a separation of the anecdotes into separate paragraphs would have made the essay a bit easier to follow along. Structure aside, this essay speaks to Allison's personal growth as the "big sister" to her older brother.

—Claire Lee

LIAM CORRIGAN

Hometown: Old Lyme, Connecticut, USA
High School: Public school, 90 students in graduating class
Ethnicity: White
Gender: Male
GPA: 4.0 out of 4.0
SAT: Reading 760, Math 790, Writing 710
ACT: n/a
SAT Subject Tests Taken: U.S. History, Physics, Literature
Extracurriculars: Varsity Crew Captain, Basketball Captain, High School Band First Trumpet, FIRST robotics, Model United Nations Club cofounder
Awards: National Honor Society, Hartford Courant Scholar athlete, U.S. Rowing Youth Olympic Team, Louis Armstrong Jazz Award, Shoreline Conference Scholar Athlete
Major: Astrophysics

ESSAY

I sat in a pair at the starting line for the repechage of the 1000 meter rowing race at the Youth Olympic Games in Nanjing, China. I had trained all summer, twice a day, six days a week, for this level of international competition. The only problem was that I had done all of this training in the eight, in preparation for Junior Worlds, so I had relatively little experience both rowing and steering in the pair, the boat I was rowing here. Sitting at the starting line, however, I wasn't nervous. I should have been nervous; this was a big deal. But I was not. I was beyond excited. I had the opportunity to win a real Olympic gold medal. I had trained as hard as my competition. I knew that I was as fast on the erg as my competitors. Then, the announcer began calling the countries, "Egypt, Romania, Italy, U.S.A., Turkey, Slovenia." I heard, "Attention," and seconds later, the light turned green, the starting beep sounded, and the race began.

At 200 meters, looking to my sides, I realized we were doing well, leading even. This could be a race. Suddenly, though, we were extremely close to the buoy line and in attempting to steer toward the middle of the lane, we caught a crab. My oar became stuck deep in the water causing me to lose control. As the oar swung over my head, I had a moment of clarity. As many times as I had visualized the race in preparation, I had never imagined such a complete loss of control. At the starting line, I was hoping for a fast, clean race. Minutes later, I had revised my aspirations, hoping that we would not be last by more than ten seconds. We wove erratically down the course, bouncing from the left to the right buoy lines. Eventually, in the last 250 meters, we ended up in a different lane. My pair partner shook with rage and frustration. The race was seemingly endless. I heard the buzzer as the first place boat crossed the finish line, and an agonizing seventeen seconds later, we finally finished. I was nearly crying, sadness and guilt had overcome me. My partner was swearing, furious. This failure was my fault. I was steering. But the real obstacle was not the failure, but that in spite of the failure, we had to come back the next day and race another race.

Everyone has experienced failure to some degree, and everyone has had to overcome it, but the emotion, the abysmal feeling which I experienced during and after that race, were entirely new to me. In truth, the situation was not dire. This failure was not life or death, but perhaps this is precisely why I was so scared of what I felt. I did not know that such an emotion could be generated from something as innocuous as a crew race; but, I was representing the United States of America, I was representing the program and the coaches for which I had rowed, and I was representing myself. I had failed them all. But I would still go home and eat a proper meal. I would get a good night's sleep on a mattress. My life would go on, virtually unchanged. Nonetheless, I felt as if the world were crashing down around me. I needed to change this. I needed to overcome this, and in order to do so I could not give up. I had to come back the next day and succeed, doing the same thing at which I had failed the day before. Ultimately, I discovered why failure is so trying. It is not the failure itself. That is only a moment of pain in your life that will be over soon enough. Instead, it is the fact that in spite of failure, you must persevere, no matter how bleak things may be, and hopefully, one day you will succeed. Along with each success will come many failures, but you must try your best to endure and overcome these obstacles time and again.

REVIEW

Students are often warned against writing their personal statements about sports, the logic being that most of these essays read similarly: the student establishes his or her aspirations to greatness at the beginning of the essay. By the end, they have learned that spectacular achievements are within reach but require discipline and commitment. In triumphant fashion, Liam turns the infamous Sports Essay on its head, skipping a retelling of his ascent to greatness, instead beginning his narrative there—at the Youth Olympics—and promptly recounting what he considers to be utter and total failure. There's no saccharine-sweet success-against-all-odds discussion here.

Though there are moments in this essay where the turn of phrase could be streamlined or clearer, the piece communicates an astounding amount about its writer both in its content and execution. We obviously learn that Liam is a talented rower and disciplined athlete. More broadly, we glean a sense of self-deprecating humor, or at least a healthy dose of perspective, in his ability to write so candidly and energetically about what was imaginably a hugely disappointing experience.

As well, Liam's move to conclude his essay by drawing an important life lesson from his time at the Olympics is a stellar one. It speaks to his maturity and ability to reflect, and it effectively renders this much more than a "Sports Essay" after all.

—Lily K. Calcagnini

ESME TRAHAIR

Hometown: London, United Kingdom
High School: Private school, 164 students in graduating class
Ethnicity: White and Black
Gender: Female
GPA: 4.9 out of 5.0
SAT: Reading 800, Math 800, Writing 800
ACT: n/a
SAT Subject Tests Taken: Mathematics Level 2, Chemistry, French
Extracurriculars: Editor in chief and founder of school newspaper, varsity girls Swim captain, musician (oboe and piano), Duke of Edinburgh Gold Award participant
Awards: Oboe ABRSM Performance Diploma, ACS Cobham Founder's Award, Presidential Scholar semifinalist, National Honor's Society, IB Diploma
Major: Social Anthropology

ESSAY

Ten minutes before my orchestra and I were due to perform what would be my first symphony, our conductor called us into the wings of the stage for a pep talk. He told us how hard we had all worked, and I could tell that he was struggling to say something that would truly inspire a group of excited twelve and thirteen year olds. After about six minutes of clichés, he looked at his watch and hurriedly delivered his closing line: "One day, you'll reach a point where you don't get nervous anymore."

A point where you don't get nervous anymore.

That night, I embarked on a mission to find that point. I've performed at concert halls, churches, and venues all over the U.K. I've played as a soloist and as part of an ensemble to packed audiences. I've auditioned for seats in orchestras and for conservatories. I've performed at examinations on three different instruments. And yet, this point eludes me, the point at which I no longer feel my own anxiety, worries, and doubts about the performance I am about to give. I have yet to reach this magical and amazing place. And recently, I decided to stop looking.

I gave up my quest for this "point" during a concert with my orchestra. We were performing a piece by Debussy, one I had fallen in love with as soon as I played it. I was the first-chair oboist, and toward the end of the piece is an oboe solo; completely exposed, extremely difficult to play, and powerful enough to render the entire performance either incredible or mediocre. Needless to say, I was so nervous that I was sure that members of the audience could hear my frantic breathing onstage as we drew closer to the solo, measure by measure. As I took a breath to begin playing, I closed my eyes and thought of all hours I had practiced, all tiny details I needed to remember while playing, all of the amazing performances I had heard. I thought of how transcendent and haunting I wanted it to sound, how I wanted every member of the audience to freeze and just listen. And I played it. Every note sounded exactly as I imagined it, and every pitch released another burst of adrenaline in my body. As the solo came to a close, the entire orchestra launched into the finale, filling the concert hall with a sound so rich and powerful I felt that I was going to burst. As I sustained the last note of the piece with the 80 other musicians on stage, I thought, "Why would you ever want to reach a point without nerves, when overcoming nervousness delivers so much?"

I stopped looking for a place without anxiety because I realized that this "point" was really just code for a place of apathy. I thought I was looking for a state of being in which I would be entirely professional and calm, but I discovered that it is the on-edge feelings and challenges that sharpen me and make my performance worthwhile, and the wide range of emotions that make a performance incredible. I am convinced that this is true of life in general, and whether I'm swimming in a race, completely in tune with my environment, taking a test where I feel confident and prepared, or playing my instruments in performance; I never forget that I am in a race, an exam, or a performance, and the result reflects hours of preparation and hard work. In music and in life it is important to recognize and remember that while a place of serenity and competence seems appealing, to reach it would render every aspect of life mundane, numb, and ordinary. By contrast, pushing oneself to do better, to play better, to be better makes hard-earned accomplishments and experiences memorable. And if the price for excellence is a little anxiety, I am more than willing to pay it.

REVIEW

The biggest strength of Esme's essay is its acknowledgment and acceptance of her vulnerabilities. Namely, her nervousness. She confounds the reader's first impressions by shifting the focus of her essay to the importance of that very nervous feeling she initially feared. By tracing the evolution of her feelings toward nervousness using a single dynamic example (her solo), Esme takes the reader on the journey with her, thus creating a connection with the reader.

By centering her discussion of her musical accomplishment around the theme of nervousness, Esme avoids a common mistake among college essay writers. Oftentimes, high school seniors are tempted to merely rehash their résumé in their application essays, but successful essays, like Esme's, drill deep into one accomplishment. Through it, we get concrete examples of her industriousness (those "hours of preparation and hard work" before the oboe solo) and her artistic sensibilities. In this way, she follows the first rule uttered by almost every writing teacher: Show, don't tell.

Esme's essay does three things well: it charts a progression (a quest to avoid nervousness turns into a sort of reverence for it), it takes the reader along for that progression using vivid narrative, and it illustrates her musical passion without being obvious about it.

—Ramsey Fahs and Julia DeBenedictis

ELIZA ALTON

Hometown: Binghamton, New York, USA
High School: Public school, 320 students in graduating class
Ethnicity: Biracial
Gender: Female
GPA: 103 out of 100
SAT: Reading 690, Math 700, Writing 730
ACT: n/a
SAT Subject Tests Taken: n/a
Extracurriculars: Cheerleading, vice president of student government, treasurer of French club, member of National Honor Society
Awards: None
Major: Environmental Science and Public Policy

ESSAY

The event that has most impacted my life and shaped my identity was my mother's life and death. My mother and I never had a conventional relationship. However, we did share a special mother daughter bond.

Because of my mother's life and death I am more tolerant. I have a different view now on what determines a person's worth and I am a changed person. I believe it is a change for the better.

My relationship with my mother was unconventional and often challenging. I had not lived with my mother since I was two years old. She knew she could not give me all the things she wanted for me in life, so unselfishly, she allowed my grandmother to raise me.

She was often in and out of my life, but I always knew how much she loved me. She was always ill; she had bipolar disorder and an array of other illnesses ranging from addiction to leukemia.

I was often embarrassed by her and our relationship. However, as I began to mature, I came to understand more about her illnesses. Consequently I was able to better understand the impact of illness, mental or physical, others might be experiencing. Because of my embarrassment and confusion, I made it so very few people knew about my mother's situation. I eventually came to realize how many people do not understand the struggles in the lives of others. This realization made me realize the importance of being tolerant of others and being sensitive to what they might be experiencing in their lives.

A few weeks after my mother's death I was asked the question: "Is a person's worth determined by professional success or acquired wealth?" I realized that many people in our society believe that a person's worth is determined by their success and wealth. My mother never graduated high school, she never attended college, and she never had a real job or career, despite her vast intelligence. After her death I was amazed at the influx of people who informed me that my mother was a wonderful person with the biggest and most caring heart they had ever known; how they admired her sense of humor, her affectionate manner, and her capacity to love.

She truly was a remarkable person, not because of a career or money but because of her character. Reflecting on the question, I found myself thinking of Martin Luther King's "I Have a Dream" speech in which he stated "people should be judged not on the color of their skin, but the quality of their character." I believe that character is one of the most important measures of a person's worth.

I now realize that what I want most in life is to make a difference in peoples' lives the way my mother did for me and others. I am extremely grateful to my mother for her role in shaping my identity and my view of the world.

REVIEW

From the beginning, Eliza makes it clear that she is going to talk about a big topic: the impact that her mother's life and death both had on her. This sort of essay topic is tricky because, although it provides plentiful opportunities for her to showcase how she has matured as a person, she needs to avoid being too vague about how specifically she has changed. Through this essay, the reader gradually learns more and more about Eliza's mother, which helps guide the reader in understanding how Eliza's own views toward her mother and her friends have changed. In this essay, the dynamic growth of Eliza's understanding is the key to the natural flow of the essay.

That being said, Eliza's introduction does seem a bit repetitive in emphasizing how "unconventional" her relationship with her mother was. If she were able to condense the first seven sentences, it is possible that she could have used that space to dig in deeper into specific examples of how Eliza misjudged or came to better understand her mother. Alternatively, she could have used that space to better bridge the transition from her recognizing the importance of people's character to her realizing that she most wanted to work like her mother to make a difference in people's lives.

—M. Hanl Park

V. EXPERIENCES ABROAD

According to Harvard College admissions statistics, about 11 percent of admitted students are from outside the United States. Though getting into Harvard as an international applicant is very competitive, experience abroad can successfully set international students apart. Importantly, growing up in a different part of the world gives the applicant distinct life experiences that can be conveyed through the college essay better than it can be described in any other part of the application.

In this section, read about a student from Kazakhstan discussing the stigma against women in her society and how she's tried to defy stereotypes of women, and learn about how a student from Russia juxtaposes his parents' struggle through the Vietnam Communist upheaval against his love of information technology and the sense of freedom it brings.

These international stories showcase the students' cultural customs and experiences that are vastly different from American norms to make the essay truly unique in the eyes of admissions officers. Despite its international focus, all applicants can learn from the key takeaways in this section: Students use evocative details of their home life—sights, sounds, smells—to draw a full picture of their pre-college life and how that upbringing shaped who they are today.

ALEXANDRA TODOROVA

Hometown: Gorna Oryahovitsa, Bulgaria
High School: Public school, 30 students in graduating class
Ethnicity: White
Gender: Female
GPA: 6.0 out of 6.0
SAT: Reading 730, Math 760, Writing 800
ACT: n/a
SAT Subject Tests Taken: Literature, World History
Extracurriculars: Tennis player, coordinator and volunteer in the Gorna Oryahovitsa Youth Parliament (non-governmental organization), class president and member of the student council, editor in chief of the high school newspaper
Awards: Living Rainforest Essay Competition finalist in Sustainability Debate, third place in Literary Essay Competition "Jews and Bulgarians—Two Nations, One Country, One Love," first place in Bulgaria si ti! English competition, third place in English Language Olympiad organized by the Bulgarian Ministry of Education and Science, third place in Bilingual English/Russian competition organized by the Bulgarian Ministry of Education and Science
Major: Social Anthropology

ESSAY

As a child raised on two continents, my life has been defined by the "What if . . . ?" question. What if I had actually been born in the

United States? What if my parents had not won that Green card? What if we had stayed in the USA and had not come back to Bulgaria? These are the questions whose answers I will never know (unless, of course, they invent a time machine by 2050).

"Born in Bulgaria, lived in Orlando, Florida, currently lives in Bulgaria" is what I always write in the About Me section of an Internet profile. Hidden behind that short statement is my journey of discovering where I belong.

My parents moved to the United States when I was two years old. For the next four years it was my home country. I was an American. I fell in love with Dr. Seuss books and the PBS Kids TV channel, Twizzlers and pepperoni, Halloweens and Thanksgivings, the yellow school bus and the "Good job!" stickers.

It took just one day for all of that to disappear. When my mother said "We are moving back to Bulgaria," I naïvely asked, "Is that a town or a state?"

Twenty hours later I was standing in the middle of an empty room, which itself was in the middle of an unknown country.

It was then that the "what if"—my newly imagined adversary— made its first appearance. It began to follow me on my way to school. It sat right behind me in class. No matter what I was doing, I could sense its ubiquitous presence.

The "what if" slowly took its time over the years. Just when it seemed to have faded away, it reappeared resuming its tormenting influence on me—a constant reminder of all that could have been. What if I had won that national competition in the United States? What if I had joined a Florida tennis club? What if I had become a part of an American non-governmental organization? Would I value my achievements more if I had continued riding on that yellow school bus every morning?

But something—at first unforeseen and vastly unappreciated— gradually worked its way into my heart and mind loosening the tight grip of the "what if"—Bulgaria. I rediscovered my home country—hours spent in the library reading about Bulgaria's history spreading over fourteen centuries, days reading books and comparing the Glagolitic and Cyrillic scripts, years traveling to some of the most remote corners of my country. It was a cathartic experience and with it finally came the discovery and acceptance of who I am.

I no longer feel the need to decide where I belong. I am like a football fan that roots for both teams during the game. (If John Isner ever plays a tennis match against Grigor Dimitrov, I will definitely be like that fan.) Bulgaria and the USA are not mutually exclusive. Instead, they complement each other in me, whether it be through incorporating English words in my daily speech, eating my American pancakes with Bulgarian white brine cheese, or still having difficulty communicating through gestures (we Bulgarians are notoriously famous for shaking our heads side to side when we mean "yes" and nodding to mean "no").

As a child raised on two continents, my life will be defined by the "What . . . ?" question. What have Bulgaria and the USA given me? What can I give them back? What does the future hold for me? This time, I will not need a time machine to find the answers I am seeking.

REVIEW

Alexandra's essay elaborates on key themes of identity as an American and Bulgarian, scholar and tennis player, and answers questions the reader will have about her extracurricular passions and motivations.

The essay is a variation on the classic college essay theme where a potential hardship becomes a positive. Here, she tells the story of overcoming a life lived in constant contemplation of hypotheticals to one where duality not a source of confusion, but one that "complements" each other. Alexandra's essay suggests that she has transcended distinction and demonstrates maturity with an ability to appreciate the quirks of both her American and Bulgarian identities.

Alexandra's "rediscovery" of her home country serves as an opportunity for her to mention her interests and hobbies, providing context and narrative support for the extracurricular activities she probably lists on her application. Speaking about Bulgarian history, travels, and code switching, Alexandra conveys a cultural awareness and keen observation of nuance in her essay.

Alexandra's essay could have used a bit more of thorough examination of how her "rediscovery" translated to her ultimate response to the "what if" question. It takes a distinct experience—splitting a childhood between two vastly different worlds—but doesn't go far enough in exploring the process behind her transformation to make her story of self-discovery truly substantive or original.

—Wonik Son

NURIYA SAIFULINA

Hometown: Astana, Kazakhstan
High School: Public school, 90 students in graduating class
Ethnicity: White
Gender: Female
GPA: 4.0 out of 4.0
SAT: Reading 760, Math 740, Writing 800
ACT: n/a
SAT Subject Tests Taken: Mathematics Level 2, Literature
Extracurriculars: Main actress in city's drama club, founder of a feminist book club, member of EducationUsa, independent volunteer, artist
Awards: First place in city's geometry Olympiad, second and third place math Olympiad, first place Russian language Olympiad, first places in numerous English competitions (city and regional)
Major: Economics

ESSAY

Growing up in a society in which any sign of femininity is associated with poor intelligence and lack of logic, I have had people frequently doubting my abilities and discouraging me from pursuing my academic goals. "After all, you are a girl. You cannot understand economics!" "Do not worry about math too much: you will not need it to be a good wife." These voices never stop, no matter how hard I try to prove my worth. The fault is probably mine: I mean, I am asking for all the sexist remarks, am I not? I am so silly dyeing my hair blond and wearing pink lip gloss. I could easily make myself seem more intelligent by concealing my femininity, but I would rather spend time trying to become smart than trying to look smart. After all, does it really matter if a person studying intensely and working hard is a woman or if she is wearing sparkling eyeshadow instead of thick glasses?

I decided that no unspoken sexist "rules" of my society will ever turn me away from my interests and goals, and I absolutely love the path I have chosen. I join "manly" conversations about economy, despite the condescending snorts. I decorate my trusty TI-84 with rhinestones and buy cute pink stationery to beat the SATs with. I participate in all academic competitions I can, and even win some of them despite lacking a certain member. My teachers, friends, and even family may believe that I am "just a girl," but I know that my persistence to defy stereotypes and achieve my goal of receiving quality education will show other girls that they can achieve more than society thinks.

After the prestigious geometry Olympiad is over I, the captain of the winning team, smile with my new shiny medal on my chest, and some guy from the opposing team comes up to me and starts a conversation: "You are kind of smart for a girl." With the brightest smile I answer: "I bet you wish you could be as smart as a girl too."

REVIEW

Nuriya effectively uses her essay as a space to convey aspects of her personality—namely, her femininity and the unapologetic zeal with which she asserts it. Her choice to begin with an anecdote about getting ready in the bathroom for an Olympiad competition is a wise one. Just subtle enough, the mirror motif immediately makes clear Nuriya's purpose: to draw a distinction between the young woman she sees and the one that her sexist society does.

The essay's structure is a textbook example of narrative organization. After introducing us to the stereotypes that people (including her own mother!) assign her, Nuriya spends a couple of paragraphs explaining exactly how she's defied such prejudice. Nuriya's insertion of specific details—her dream to become a financial analyst and the rhinestones with which she adorns her TI-84—make her appear a more personable and endearing character. The reader understands well that Nuriya possesses conviction in herself and her choices, whether to dye her hair blond or eschew thick eyeglasses for "sparkling eye shadow." Nuriya's greatest strength lies, then, in the emphatic tone with which she depicts her poise through years of pushback from those judging on cursory and superficial impressions.

In ending Nuriya not only coheres her writing around a central event, but also adds a layer of complexity to the mirror motif that she earlier introduced: She is both the girl applying makeup and, having won the competition, the girl wearing a "new shiny metal" strapped to her chest. Ultimately, Nuriya leaves the reader feeling inspired and convinced that she will continue to resist naysayers as she faces more challenges in the years ahead.

—Aisha Bhoori

NICOLAS YAN

Hometown: Auckland, New Zealand
High School: Private school, 208 students in graduating class
Ethnicity: Asian
Gender: Male
GPA: n/a (school does not calculate)
SAT: Reading 800, Math 780, Writing 780
ACT: n/a
SAT Subject Tests Taken: Literature, U.S. History
Extracurriculars: Crew varsity coxswain, student newspaper editor, Student Government House prefect, InZone Foundation student tutor
Awards: 2015 the *Atlantic* & College Board Writing Grand Prize, Russell McVeagh Law Scholarship, Victoria University Excellence Scholarship
Major: Undecided

ESSAY

When I failed math in my sophomore year of high school, a bitter dispute engulfed my household—"Nicolas Yan vs. Mathematics." I was the plaintiff, appearing *pro se*, while my father represented the defendant (inanimate as it was). My brother and sister constituted a rather understaffed jury, and my mother presided over the case as judge.

In a frightening departure from racial stereotype, I charged Mathematics with the capital offences of being "too difficult" and "irrelevant to my aspirations," citing my recent shortcomings in the subject as evidence. My father entered a not guilty plea on the defendant's behalf, for he had always harbored hopes that I would follow in his entrepreneurial footsteps—and who ever heard of a businessman who wasn't an accomplished mathematician? He argued that because I had fallen sick before my examination and had been unable to sit one of the papers, it would be a travesty of justice to blame my "Ungraded" mark on his client. The judge nodded sagely.

With heartrending pathos, I recalled how I had studied A-Level Mathematics with calculus a year before the rest of my cohort, bravely grappling with such perverse concepts as the *poisson* distribution to no avail. I decried the subject's lack of real-life utility and lamented my inability to reconcile further effort with any plausible success; so that to persist with Mathematics would be a Sisyphean endeavor. Since I had no interest in becoming the entrepreneur that my father envisioned, I petitioned the court for academic refuge in the humanities. The members of the jury exchanged sympathetic glances and put their heads together to deliberate.

In hushed tones, they weighed the particulars of the case. Then, my sister announced their unanimous decision with magisterial gravity: "Nicolas shouldn't have to do math if he doesn't want to!" I was ecstatic; my father distraught. With a bang of her metaphorical gavel, the judge sentenced the defendant to "Death by Omission"—and so I chose my subjects for 11th Grade *sans* Mathematics. To my father's disappointment, a future in business for me now seemed implausible.

Over the next year, however, new evidence that threw the court's initial verdict into question surfaced. Languishing on death row, Mathematics exercised its right to appeal, and so our quasi-court reconvened in the living room.

My father reiterated his client's innocence, maintaining that Mathematics was neither "irrelevant" nor "too difficult." He proudly recounted how just two months earlier, when my friends had convinced me to join them in creating a business case competition for high school students (clerical note: the loftily-titled New Zealand Secondary Schools Case Competition), I stood in front of the Board of a company and successfully pitched them to sponsor us—was this not evidence that I could succeed in business? I think I saw a tear roll down his cheek as he implored me to give Mathematics another chance.

I considered the truth of his words. While writing a real-world business case for NZSSCC, I had been struck by how mathematical processes actually *made sense* when deployed in a practical context, and how numbers could tell a story just as vividly as words can. By reviewing business models and comparing financial projections to actual returns, one can read a company's story and identify areas of potential growth; whether the company then took advantage of these opportunities determined its success. It wasn't that my role in organizing NZSSCC had magically taught me to embrace all things mathematical or commercial—I was still the same person—but I recognized that no intellectual constraints prevented me from succeeding in Mathematics; I needed only the courage to seize an opportunity for personal growth.

I stood up and addressed my family: "I'll do it." Then, without waiting for the court's final verdict, I crossed the room to embrace my father: and the rest, as they (seldom) say, was Mathematics.

REVIEW

Nicolas opens this essay by doing what some might see as unthinkable: admitting that he failed a math class in high school. In light of the fact that colleges would almost certainly already have this information, this topic fits perfectly into the Common Application prompt about a background that is "so meaningful . . . their application would be incomplete without it." Just as crucial as his selection of a topic, however, is his decision to frame the piece as a trial for math itself. But even then, he avoids the obvious route of making himself the defendant and chooses to put math on trial. In a surprising twist, he wins his case and is allowed to drop math, much to the dismay of his father. Of course, the most effective part of the essay subtly explains that the story does not end there. The appeal that follows the initial verdict is both creative and effective, showing an important personal transformation for the writer.

This essay is a great example of what happens when the writer takes a risk that pays off. Starting by admitting failure and then putting math "on trial" is not a typical framework for a college essay. But Nicolas's essay is effective precisely because it is not typical. It is both deeply personal and unique. Indeed, the writer perfectly answers the prompt, providing a meaningful story that places his application in a new context.

—Ryan O'Meara

THOMAS CHATZIELEFTHERIOU

Hometown: Mytilene, Lesvos, Greece
High School: Public school, 43 students in graduating class
Ethnicity: White
Gender: Male
GPA: 4.0 out of 4.0
SAT: Reading 730, Math 780, Writing 750
ACT: n/a
SAT Subject Tests Taken: Mathematics Level 2, World History, Latin
Extracurriculars: President of Student Council, member of the Mytilene Tennis Club, leading actor of the high school drama club, founding member of the New Mytilene Philharmonic Orchestra, participant in the Comenius EU Student Exchange Program
Awards: Bronze Medal in the National Mathematics Olympiad, Diploma of Merit in the National Philosophical Essay Contest, Diploma of Distinction in the National Young Business Talents Economics Competition, Diploma of Merit for the Highest GPA in Class, first place in the essay contest for the selection of the Greek team in the Euroscola Program of the EU Parliament
Major: Social Studies

ESSAY

It all began one day in June 2004. It was the end of the school year and everything was covered in a veil of idleness. For my classmates, this season of chirping cicadas was a time for games by the sea. Not for me. I just wanted to bury my nose in my books and devour the

Atlas of Empires I had recently acquired. My electronic encyclopedia would come next, and anything else that would give me the one thing I most desired: knowledge.

While flying with the wings of imagination, my mother came to me and lovingly said: "Now that you are older, it's time you learnt more about your grandparents' place, which is why we decided to vacation in the village." My sobs still echo in my ears as I stir up the recollections lost in the depths of my memory. Although I had travelled to the ends of the earth through the pages of *National Geographic*, never before had I left my comfortable corner for long. I was afraid, but the decision was final.

Before long I found myself in the waters of a wonderful new world, but I did not rush to enjoy the freshness of its revitalizing currents. Instead, I naively asked grandpa: "Where's the library?" He looked into my eyes and said: "Out there. I may not know much, but remember these words: read as much as you like and make me proud, but don't forget that the greatest book is the world around you, the one you must understand and feel." He then took me by the hand and led me to the neighborhood square where the children were playing and said: "Live your childhood now, before it's too late."

This was my first encounter with a different philosophy of life. I found it strange how those children, free of any anxieties, turned every second of their time into a spontaneous ode to joy. Eventually I was allured by this newfound carefree spirit. I allowed myself to have fun and twirl in the energy of restless companionship. This is more or less how I spent that summer, and the summers after, each of them an oasis of relief that gave me the necessary strength to get through the following year.

Idleness never got the better of us; were always coming up with imaginative ways to make use of our creative bent. We sat under the Aegean sun and watched the boats entering and leaving the port; we built humble wooden shelters, explored abandoned mansions and held our own Olympic Games, using ribbons as prizes and barrels as podia. We felt the pulse of nature and wandered paths in the countryside, united always by the bonds of solidarity and a sense of collectiveness.

Nothing is the same anymore. Now slaves to the conventions of adult society, some work to help their parents and others, tormented by the inhumane examination system, are striving to get into university. I am certain, however, that a new and better chapter in life filled with experiences, intellectual challenges and cosmopolitism is about to open. But I cannot help but wonder what happened to the halcyon days at my childhood haven in Arcadia. Did they die?

The answer is no. They live within me, as an integral part of the mystery known as the human spirit. How could their invaluable teachings be lost? They have taught me to respect diversity, engage in dialogue with it, demonstrate sportsmanship, build relationships on trust and share in the joys and sorrows of my fellows. I learned to appreciate the value of *aurea mediocritas* before learning about it from Aristotle, and realized that man is a *plus que machine*, before learning about it from the thinkers of the French Enlightenment. Above all, I now devote myself to something because I love it and not because I expect to gain from it. In the end, grandpa was right.

REVIEW

Thomas uses this essay to highlight his intellectual curiosity, his descriptive writerly talent, and his awareness of how learning occurs in a variety of different ways. These are three key attributes a college might look for in its potential students. The piece makes two turns (a realistic number for an admissions reader to track): the first from a youthful preference for bookish knowledge toward the experiential learning he discovers on the summer vacations; the second to reconcile that new interest with societal constraints that value only conventional learning. In doing so, Thomas offers a subtle challenge to the workaholic, high-achieving culture that is motivating other, perhaps less authentic, essays and resumes submitted by others. That critique could come off as shrill or self-righteous, but by anchoring his position in an earnest childhood memory, it seems entirely authentic.

One can imagine how well this essay might fit into a broader application: highlighting how Thomas's summer résumé items were more personal than preprofessional; demonstrating how his academic achievements are inflected with an inherent passion. We see that connection illustrated in the essay's brilliant close, in which Thomas uses a set of parallel constructions to unify his intellectual Greek and French studies with the experiential knowledge he treasured in those childhood summers.

—Colton Valentine

Ryan Voon

Hometown: Hong Kong SAR
High School: Private school, 83 students in graduating class
Ethnicity: Asian
Gender: Male
GPA: 90 out of 100
SAT: n/a
ACT: n/a
SAT Subject Tests Taken: n/a
Extracurriculars: Varsity squash captain, school newspaper colum-
  nist, philosophy club founder, debate club member
Awards: George Livingston Nichols Prize, awarded to the student
  with the best essay on a historical topic; The Emerson Prize (2014)
  by the *Concord Review* for excellence in research and writing on
  a historical topic.
Major: Government and Economics

ESSAY

"I don't understand. You are not Buddhist, but you spend so much
time studying Buddhism." I have often heard this statement, but coming from a monk at the renowned Shwedegon Pagoda in Yangon,
Myanmar, it resonated more deeply. I was conducting field research
for an internship with the University of Toronto, and the supervis-
ing professor had tasked me with interviewing monks and pilgrims
at the holy site. In the past 2 years, I have engaged in four research

projects regarding Buddhism—reading sociology reports, summarizing research papers and transcribing Sanskrit texts—but this was the first internship that required me to interact with practicing Buddhists, not just Buddhist academics. The experience would cement my commitment to understand Buddhist philosophy and history, and confirm my desire to continue my study of Buddhism in college.

I've always enjoyed reading about history, especially how societies transformed themselves, whether through war and conquest like the Mongol Empire, or through culture and assimilation like Ancient Greece. The more I read, the more I realized the importance of religious convictions that motivated men and women to accomplish historic achievements—the Pilgrims who endured the winters of hardship to build a new world, the British evangelists who led the global fight for abolishing slavery or the Arab merchants who spread Islam as eagerly as they established valuable trade routes. I did not need to share their beliefs to appreciate how faith shaped their actions. As an American growing up in Asia, and after reading books such as Dr. Robert Thurman's *The Jewel Tree of Tibet*, I became fascinated by the way Buddhism helped to transform the great warlike Asoka, Tibetan, and Mongol empires into societies emphasizing peace and harmony. This fascination led me to internships with the American Institute of Buddhism to understand better the beliefs of Mahayana doctrine on Tibetan culture and later with the Gandhari Project team at the University of Munich to learn about the spread of Buddhism in ancient Central Asia.

While I enjoyed these learning opportunities, the research I conducted at the Shwedegon opened my eyes to the relevance of Buddhism in the daily lives of people today. Every day for one month, I stayed for hours at the huge temple complex (the perimeter of which takes about 45 minutes to walk around), watching rituals and gatherings and documenting my observations. My favorite activity was sitting among the *sangha* (the community of adherents), documenting my observations of discussions that a group of three monks regularly presided over at a side pavilion. In my most memorable encounter, I watched as a middle-aged mother sought advice about her daughter who was considering an abortion. The monks discussed the principle of *ahiṃsā* (non-violence) and how it applied as well to the unborn. But rather than simply instructing her what to do, they also explained that the *gandhabba* (the consciousness waiting to be reborn) may arise only several months after conception, thus implicitly permitting early-stage abortions. I sensed no arrogance and no air of superiority from the monks as they discussed these principles, appearing to trust the woman herself to apply these concepts in her own way. I was moved by the simple compassion they showed the woman and recall the deep sympathy and respect I felt for the mother as she struggled to make the "right" decision, even as her advisors could not give a definitive answer.

I did not challenge the senior monk who questioned why I should be studying Buddhism—it was not an appropriate time—but my answer is that I want to understand the society that I live in, and that requires an understanding of the belief systems that motivate so many of us. The Shwedegon experience made me appreciate that religion not only motivates historic achievements but also inspires daily efforts. The experience has made me even more excited to continue to study and research Buddhism in college.

REVIEW

Ryan's essay begins immediately with a sort of tension and confusion, exemplified through the question posed by a figure of certain authority. And it's exactly this tension between his lack of personal experience and his passion that he explores throughout his essay. What makes him so interested in Buddhism? Why is it important to him? Ryan strives to address these questions in the couple hundred words in his essay.

It's not difficult to recognize his intellectual curiosity or his enthusiasm for social studies, and more specifically, history and religion. He describes the pieces of history that interest him, the books that have affected him, and his resulting actions; it's the perfect balance of information and of personal storytelling. He is able to convey his knowledgeability and his passion without boring the reader with trivial facts or overly technical terms. All things mentioned might be rather abstract, so Ryan leads on to the third paragraph, where things become concrete and personal. He describes beautifully an experience he had—something that made Buddhism more personal, and more prevalent, especially given its application to the controversial topic of abortion. He is honest, he is open, and he is clearly very thoughtful.

Like tying the perfect knot, Ryan returns to the same question that he began with, but this time with a very clear answer. Buddhism might not have the cut-and-dry answers he's looking for, but there is doubt that he ardently wants to look for answers nonetheless. The essay is well written, fairly succinct, and expresses the sentiments of the author effectively.

—Amy Zhao

JIAFENG CHEN

Hometown: Shanghai, China
High School: Private school, 153 students in graduating class
Ethnicity: Asian
Gender: Male
GPA: 98 out of 100
SAT: Reading 800, Math 800, Writing 800
ACT: n/a
SAT Subject Tests Taken: U.S. History, Mathematics Level 2, Biology E/M
Extracurriculars: Model United Nations founder and president; math competition president; theater, various responsibilities, 7 seasons
Awards: Best Delegate at Model United Nations conferences at Harvard and Princeton; Outstanding Delegate at Penn; AMC school champion and AIME qualifier
Major: Applied Mathematics

ESSAY

I have a fetish for writing.

I'm not talking about crafting prose or verses, or even sentences out of words. But simply constructing letters and characters from strokes of ink gives me immense satisfaction. It's not quite calligraphy, as I don't use calligraphic pens or Chinese writing brushes; I prefer it simple, spontaneous, and subconscious. I often find myself crafting characters in the margins of notebooks with a fifty-cent pencil, or tracing letters out of thin air with anything from chopsticks to fingertips.

The art of handwriting is a relic in the information era. Why write when one can type? Perhaps the Chinese had an answer before the advent of keyboards. "One's handwriting," said the ancient Chinese, "is a painting of one's mind." After all, when I practice my handwriting, I am crafting *characters*.

My character.

I particularly enjoy meticulously designing a character, stroke by stroke, and eventually building up, letter by letter, to a quote personalized in my own voice. Every movement of the pen and every droplet of ink all lead to something profound, as if the arches of every "m" are doorways to revelations. After all, characters are the building blocks of language, and language is the only vehicle through which knowledge unfolds. Thus, in a way, these letters under my pen are themselves representations of knowledge, and the delicate beauty of every letter proves, *visually*, the intrinsic beauty of knowing. I suppose handwriting reminds me of my *conviction* in this visual manner: through learning answers are found, lives enriched, and societies bettered.

Moreover, perhaps this strange passion in polishing every single character of a word delineates my dedication to learning, testifies my zeal for my conviction, and sketches a crucial stroke of my character.

"We—*must*—know . . ." the mathematician David Hilbert's voice echoes in resolute *cursive* at the tip of my pen, as he, addressing German scientists in 1930, propounds the goal of modern intellectuals. My pen firmly nods in agreement with Hilbert, while my mind again fumbles for the path to knowledge.

The versatility of handwriting enthralls me. The Chinese developed many styles—called *hands*—of writing. Fittingly, each hand seems to parallel one of my many academic interests. Characters of the Regular Hand (*kai shu*), a legible script, serve me well during many long hours when I scratch my head and try to prove a mathematical statement rigorously, as the legibility illuminates my logic on paper. Words of the Running Hand (*xing shu*), a semi-cursive script, are like the passionate words that I speak before a committee of Model United Nations delegates, propounding a decisive course of action: the words, both spoken and written, are swift and coherent but resolute and emphatic. And strokes of the Cursive Hand (*cao shu*) resemble those sudden artistic sparks when I deliver a line on stage: free, spontaneous, but emphatic syllables travel through the lights like rivers of ink flowing on the page.

Yet the fact that the three distinctive hands cooperate so seamlessly, fusing together the glorious culture of writing, is perhaps a fable of learning, a testament that the many talents of the Renaissance Man could all be worthwhile for enriching human society. Such is my methodology: just like I organize my different *hands* into a neat personal style with my fetish for writing, I can unify my broad interests with my passion for learning.

". . . We—*will*—know!" Hilbert finishes his adage, as I frantically slice an exclamation mark as the final stroke of this painting of my mind.

I must know: for knowing, like well-crafted letters, has an inherent beauty and an intrinsic value. *I will* know: for my versatile interests in academics will flow like my versatile styles of writing.

I must know and I *will* know: for my fetish for writing is a fetish for learning.

REVIEW

In his personal essay, Jiafeng describes his passion for writing, linking how he crafts letters and Chinese characters with his insatiable thirst for knowledge and how he molds his identity. The essay succeeds in using vivid verbs, clever language, and imagery to tackle this subject, providing essay readers with insight into some aspects of Jiafeng's personality: dedication, diligence, patience, and persistence.

While the essay incorporates quotations, adage, and other Chinese- and English-language snippets, mirroring the additive process of writing that Jiafeng describes, the piece would have benefitted from more personal authorial anecdotes. His words could have packed a greater punch if he had given the reader a glimpse into his specific world, rather than simply outlining the major takeaway points.

The writing at times comes across as too directed, heavy-handed and a bit too impersonal. Indeed, many prospective college applicants find solace in reading and writing. What aspects of this story could derive solely from Jiafeng? How can he jump from the page and reveal who he is, rather than merely situating himself among the words he shapes? The end of the essay's focus on different styles of Chinese handwriting begins to focus on tackling those questions, and Jiafeng could have deepened his exploration into why he loves to write by expanding that section and, perhaps, by moving it toward the top of his piece.

—Melissa Rodman

Truong Nam Nguyen Huy

Hometown: Moscow, Russia
High School: Public school, 176 students in graduating class
Nationality: Vietnamese
Gender: Male
GPA: 4.6 out of 5.0
SAT: Reading 800, Math 800, Writing 780
ACT: n/a
SAT Subject Tests Taken: Mathematics Level 2, Physics
Extracurriculars: Creator and instructor of summer programming courses for Vietnamese students in Russia, Participants' spokesperson of the summer camp for "Trai He 2014" for overseas Vietnamese students, president of EducationUSA Competitive College Club for Russian students who want to apply to colleges in the U.S., programmer of a translation software company VieGrid, winner and participant of Actions for Earth Global Youth Summit 2014
Awards: First place (twice) in Open Olympiad in Programming for students from former USSR countries, first place (twice) in Russian National Olympiad in team programming, second place (three times) in Russian National Olympiad in Informatics, first place (twice) in International Mathematical Tournament of Towns, first place in Moscow Math Olympiad
Major: Computer Science

ESSAY

When I think about a possible future in information technology, I think first about the past, when my parents endured oppression, when I was raised in false freedom.

The story of my parents' struggles during the Vietnamese Communist upheaval still disturbs me today. In the 1970s, the Communist Party forced my father into the army and confiscated the assets of my mother's aristocratic family, leaving them in utter poverty. In this desperate and dangerous environment, my parents had to be ruthless and cynical to survive, setting aside higher ideals and principles.

Though he hated the Communist Party, my father joined it in 1981 to escape the army and get a government job. And 1993, when my father won a government scholarship to study in Russia, we emigrated. There, my family achieved a sort of freedom. Unconstrained by the Vietnamese government, my father co-founded a small clothing factory, rented a one-bedroom apartment, and sent my sister and me to prominent Russian schools.

To some, this story may seem to end happily, and indeed, I'm so grateful for our good fortune. But I've often felt uneasy about how my parents had to abandon their selflessness and concern for their community in order to seek their freedom.

My parents were no longer ruthless, but when I looked broadly at Russia and Vietnam, I saw that such material freedom can often prevent true freedom. Nowadays, due to economic liberalization, the upper classes can afford incredible luxuries, yet many of them still retain the same cynical attitudes from the communist era, fending only for themselves, their families, and their prosperity, while ignoring the rigged elections, the crackdowns on dissent, the pervasive underdevelopment. In pursuit of material freedom, they accept their mental cages.

When I first became seriously interested in IT, I sometimes wondered whether I was any different. Was I pursuing distinctions in IT only for my own gain? Is IT just another route to a mental cage? Yet as I progressed in the field, I realized the answer: No.

Without IT, I would never have experienced true freedom: the freedom to seek out and engage with uncensored opinions and shape my own perspective. IT, a field that allows for multiple solutions to the same problem, demands open discussions with friends, teachers, and university professors, all of which have helped me uncage my mind. By addressing and resolving problems with others, I now think openly and flexibly; I feel trust, compassion and concern for them.

An uncaged mind is the first step toward becoming a true citizen again. I often notice how my computer science teachers and classmates are some of the most open-minded people among educated Muscovites. When, for instance, the Kremlin mandated that our school cut math lessons and teach military education instead, we all discussed possible responses before unanimously condemning and rejecting the edict.

There are few places for such free exchange in Russia, even fewer in Vietnam. As I spend my gap year in my native country, I am saddened to see so many brilliant, industrious people, young and old, still mentally caged.

But I also see signs of hope. I have seen how IT changes people the way it changed me. Even in the living room of my Moscow apartment, I have witnessed the transformative power of IT. Last summer, when I held a basic programming course for 15 Vietnamese immigrant students, they barely talked and were hesitant to answer my questions. However, as the one-month course progressed, I saw them open up—their initial shyness faded, and they enthusiastically work together on finding unique solutions. Today, they deal with their everyday problems the same way they solved my algorithmic puzzles: by sharing opinions, compromising solutions, helping each other improve.

IT is a key to unlocking mental cages, a path to community engagement, and my goal is to put it in reach of every Vietnamese.

REVIEW

Truong weaves an engaging narrative about how studying information technology has shaped his understanding of his family's history, politics in Russia and Vietnam, and freedom. Political essays are a gamble because you never know the opinions of whoever is going to read your paper; Truong succeeds, however, by making his essay extremely personal with his anecdotes and self-reflection.

Truong's opening is very effective because he signals to the reader that he is going to talk about his hopes for the future and how his past has influenced them. He outlines his family's experiences and challenges, but then he returns to the present by talking about his concerns for those still living in Vietnam.

While he tries to present the problem of mental imprisonment that he sees in Russia and Vietnam, his criticism comes off as imperious because of his generalizations. Truong comes off his soapbox, however, by making the essay personal again by clearly laying out what he thinks freedom means and how IT has allowed him to achieve it.

Truong's example of IT students reacting to changes in the school system is vague and impersonal, but his example of leading an IT course for Vietnamese students shows how he has used his studies and passion to help his community.

By the end of his essay, Truong returns to his future and how he wants to use IT to affect change. While his declaration to free the minds of his fellow Vietnamese is grandiose, it is full of passion and determination.

—Brittany Ellis

Kristina Madjoska

Hometown: Skopje, Macedonia
High School: Private school, 78 students in graduating class
Ethnicity: White
Gender: Female
GPA: 11.7 out of 12.0
SAT: Reading 690, Math 730, Writing 710
ACT: n/a
SAT Subject Tests Taken: Mathematics Level 1, Biology E/M, World History
Extracurriculars: Student council senior president; president of the General Assembly of Model European Parliament; president of Peace Corps GLOW (Girls Leading Our World) Club; debate team; teacher for Roma community
Awards: Valedictorian; Student of the Department for French, English, and History; first team placement on National Debate Championship; Head of Delegation at International Model European Parliament, first place
Major: Neurobiology

ESSAY

The Vardar River carves its crooked way along the bisection of my hometown Skopje. Even though it might seem as if Vardar is just a body of water, to the citizens of Skopje it carries much greater social implications. Namely, the southern side of the river is populated predominantly by Christian and ethnic Macedonians, whereas the northern side is the Muslim and ethnic Albanian, Bosnian, Turkish and Roma side. Segregation has never been a policy explicitly institutionalized; however, especially after the large influx of refugees from the Bosnian and Kosovo Wars, it has been ubiquitously embraced by the citizens of Skopje. Apart from the prejudice that undoubtedly surrounds religious and linguistic differences, the people of Skopje are spatially bifurcated by their ethnic disparities. I am Macedonian, and have always lived in the Macedonian part of the city. Yet, I could never help but wonder what kind of a life there is on this Other side (in my eyes a 'hinterland'), and why there is an Other side in the first place.

Clearly, I was thrilled at the opportunity to explore the issue of de facto segregation at my TASP seminar "Race and the Limits of Law in America" at Cornell University. As my final project, I was assigned the task of researching and analyzing a case from U.S history that has markedly affected social perception of race in America. Since the politics of pure racial and spatial categorization were, for me, the most compelling and relatable aspect of U.S. racial history, I decided to produce a research response on the case of *Loving v. Virginia* (1967). Having in mind the case's broader social context (for instance, its proximity to *Brown v. Board of Education* and the Civil Rights Movement), I looked at interracial marriage as an extension to segregation—that is, a segregation of the private sphere. For me, a possible law student, it was quite exciting to see how American precedent law gives such weight to each court decision, and automatically a great deal of responsibility to the justices. Even today, the precedent of the *Loving v. Virginia* ruling is important in constructing the legal argument in favor of same-sex marriages.

Apart from looking at what law could do to regulate social and intimate relationships between individuals, I also examined what law could not do to dictate their patterns. Although from a legal point of view the court ruling in favor of the interracial marriage was a remarkable historical shift, the stigma surrounding these marriages took years, even decades, to wane. Thus, it is clear that more complex psychosocial phenomena were taking place. In that sense, what especially beheld my interest was the psychological analysis of the white perceptual field that, even after desegregation, continued to necessitate an acute line of demarcation between the races. A happy, consensual and Loving marriage between a black woman and a white man was assuredly novel and distressing to the conservative white eye. Here, I could easily draw a parallel between American and Macedonian society: in both, the privileged majority wishes to erase the racial (or ethnic) Other that disturbs their visual field. This perceptual disturbance is not necessarily intentional, yet the active and conscious removal of the foreign stimulus is what promotes spatial discrimination and segregation. I, probably one of the most tolerant Macedonians spending my days in the Macedonian part of the city, am not so used to communicating with Albanians, nor do I understand their language. Even though we share the same country, our ever-growing physical and cultural distance makes them strangers in my eyes. Indubitably so, this analysis helped me see that the more we, the Macedonian Christian and Albanian Muslim communities, isolate each other, the more simply we are disturbed by each other's presence. And as the gap between the two almost parallel communities widens, segregation will continuously pervade interreligious and interethnic relationships and marriages that are still overwhelmingly scorned by mainstream Macedonian society.

Frankly, I found my TASP research project significant in that it allowed me to maneuver the legal and social aspects of a court case, while still letting me incorporate hints of my own individuality every now and then. Between reading analytical materials and writing the paper, I simultaneously deconstructed both the very American and the very Macedonian issues of any and all sorts of segregation: historically different, yet also strikingly similar. Hence I was, even for just two weeks of my high school career, a prolific and passionate student of comparative law and sociology.

REVIEW

This essay immediately captivates the reader by introducing the reader to Kristina's hometown: Skopje. Rather than presenting a litany of facts, the writer weaves history with her own more personal thoughts, creating a more intimate narrative. Importantly, the last sentence of the introduction presents the crux of the essay: the author's thoughts on what life on "the other side" is like. A great essay should be more than just an interesting story. It must have clear organization, and the author cleverly links her own personal story with a broader purpose.

Rather than dryly reciting her academic credentials, Kristina details the reasons behind her academic endeavors. She explains what most excites her academically and hints at a possible academic career. Kristina aptly juxtaposes her past academic history with her current scholarly ambitions.

While the essay is undoubtedly strong, the author could have written a stronger conclusion. The last paragraph is somewhat repetitive, and fails to "show rather than tell." In the last sentence, Kristina exclaims that she is "a prolific and passionate student of comparative law and sociology"—a repetitive statement that is already evident in the paragraphs above. Perhaps concluding with an open-ended inquiry, or by mirroring the introduction's broader focus would have made for a more engaging ending. However, these potential improvements are minor—and fail to detract from Kristina's efforts to clearly show her intellectual curiosity.

—Ryan Voon

CANGHAO CHEN

Hometown: Suzhou, China
High School: Private school, 120 students in graduating class
Ethnicity: Asian
Gender: Male
GPA: 7.0 out of 7.0
SAT: Reading 720, Math 800, Writing 730
ACT: n/a
SAT Subject Tests Taken: Mathematics Level 2, Chemistry, Physics
Extracurriculars: Student Council of UWC USA, Far East representative, charter initiator; Chinese/Hong Kong Community at UWC USA, Chinese father; math games with children instructor; UWC USA news writer
Awards: Graduate of Excellence, Excellent Student Leader of Suzhou City
Major: Economics

ESSAY

"Few in millions can speak like us," I said to King Alonso, as his loyal chancellor Gonzalo.

Under the spotlight, I wore a fluffy, emerald robe and an exquisite, shining sword, with an artificial beard on my face and a wooden crutch in my hand. I was excitedly acting my role and performing the story, together with my classmates. When King Alonso started his monologue, I glanced at the audience: my friends, my teachers and many other visitors from the nearby community. They all gathered on this evening in the auditorium of UWC-USA to appreciate Shake-speare's famous work, *The Tempest*, played by the first-year theatre students, who had been preparing this show for months.

At the end of the performance when we the actors and actresses bowed to the audience and enjoyed the thunderous applause, I felt really proud and grateful to be a theatre student at UWC-USA.

Just eight months ago, when my academic mentor suggested that I take theatre as one of my IB courses, I hesitated a lot. As a Chinese student raised with standard Chinese education, I had doubts: could theatre possibly become part of my academics? Even so, could a non-native English speaker survive in such a speaking-oriented class? Worried and apprehensive, I joined the theatre class to "have a try." Surprisingly, I found it to be an eye-opening experience as I began to learn about different practices and practitioners of theatre, to gain professional performing skills, and to successfully collaborate with my classmates. It is in this theatre class at UWC that I am able to totally explore my potential talents in theatre, something that is repressed back home.

Theatre is deemed "irrelevant" by both Chinese high schools and Chinese parents, who believe that only natural and social sciences are the basic knowledge students should master to make a living in the future. Therefore, unless I had accomplished my academic goals set by my parents and teachers, I was discouraged from participating in any theatre shows. Even more frustrating is that the prompt and contents of the shows in Chinese high schools are so restricted that only short, comedic skits which reflect students' lives are allowed on stage. Although the opportunity was limited, I still grabbed as many chances as possible to perform, simply out of my passion to express myself and to bring joy to the audience.

The atmosphere is absolutely different at UWC; not only can the-atre be part of students' academics but also acting is respected and praised. I attain confidence and happiness through the regular study and performance of theatre, and enjoy the sense of achievement a lot after my classmates and I together made this amazing show, *The Tempest*.

For the first time, I overcame my language obstacle to master a script of Shakespeare. For the first time, I put make-up on my face and dressed in a formal theatre costume to act a role with a distinctive personality. For the first time, I sensed the power of theatre that offered me a way to experience the culture and history of Shakespeare's era. Only after *The Tempest* did I realize that theatre, to me, is as essential as natural and social sciences, for it provides me with another perspective to understand the world. Furthermore, it also demonstrates and strengthens the part of my identity which dares to take an adventure, to face a challenge, and to make a difference in the end. *The Tempest* was not just a tempest on stage, but a tempest on my heart.

I am fortunate to have this realization. Indeed, few in millions can speak like I do.

REVIEW

The essay addresses culture in all senses of the word through extremely descriptive sensory language, and an interesting perspective on the expectations of the author's family, his culture, and himself. The author subtly acknowledges a few of his positive attributes in the second paragraph, with months of preparation pointing to extreme dedication and discipline to his craft. However, the characteristic that remains central throughout the essay is the author's bravery.

He challenges the beliefs of his culture by pursuing a craft that has been deemed frivolous and unnecessary. Regardless of the author's passion, he is expected to put his academics first. But, by pushing the limits of his culture's beliefs, and overcoming numerous obstacles, including speaking English as a second language in a Shakespearian play, the author shows tremendous courage, and that he is adventurous and independent in his thoughts and actions. These attributes are important to an admissions officer, who understands that students who are willing to take risks and think for themselves are often the most successful.

Though the author provides a great deal of cultural context in his essay, and it is for the most part very well crafted, the piece loses momentum at the end. In an attempt to summarize the impact that this experience has had on the author's life, the paragraph falls short of bridging a genuine connection with the reader, because it reads like a laundry list of key points.

However, the cheeky last line refers back to the very first, ambiguous line of the essay, and leaves the reader feeling satisfied that the writing has come full circle.

—Kathleen A. Cronin

VI. CULTURAL IDENTITY

Culture—whether it be ethnic, family, religious, or geographic—is not something you can easily list on a résumé. Yet for many students, it is an integral piece of the puzzle that makes them who they are. Exploring your cultural background in your admissions essay shows the reader a side of you that they certainly would miss from the rest of your application. It also gives you the opportunity to reflect on your broader cultural experience and how it has shaped your worldview.

Many of the writers in this chapter describe a conflict between cultures past and present—from growing up in the U.S. with immigrant parents to challenging ethnic cultural norms. Where these essays really shine, though, is their description of how they have reconciled or attempted to reconcile this conflict, with themselves or with others. Through this process, the writers demonstrate that they understand the complexity of culture in their own lives and in the world around them. In this chapter, you will read stories in which students describe the meaning of the word "love" in different cultural contexts, playing jazz piano on the Sabbath, and learning a native African language. Using evocative imagery of the sights, smells, and feeling of their upbringing, these essays complete the profile of the applicant in a way that is uniquely theirs.

Razi Hecker

Hometown: Bala Cynwyd, Pennsylvania, USA
High School: Private Judaic school, 37 students in graduating class
Ethnicity: White
Gender: Male
GPA: 4.0 out of 4.0
SAT: n/a
ACT: 34
SAT Subject Tests Taken: Mathematics Level 2, Chemistry, Literature, World History, Modern Hebrew
Extracurriculars: Slam poetry captain; Jewish Youth Group president; music—two bands and three instruments; workshops in innercity working with refugees (volunteer); lead writer for qualitative research paper
Awards: Harvard Book Award, Jewish Philosophy Award, National Honors Society, Strength in Humanities Award
Major: Psychology

ESSAY

"Not everything is black and white."

My mother tells me this almost every day. But my piano begs to differ. On its 88 keys I can see the ghostly imprints of perfectly aligned fingerprints. I've played classical music for years, where wrong notes are wrong, and right notes are right. But everything changed when I discovered jazz. Now jazz . . . jazz tells a different story. When I play

"Have You Met Miss Jones," I improvise, as I am the one scripting the music, creating a conversation between two lovers. My fingers no longer imitate, they create.

My best friend Noa ran over to me, red-eyed and breathless. Her face was grim as she handed me a copy of the *Jewish Exponent*. In it was an article with snippets from our city-wide poetry slam final competition. I remember that the night we performed, our words were beautiful. They questioned gender roles and normative narratives delegated in our culture, and won us second place. The problem was that Noa and I live in a tight-knit, traditional Orthodox Jewish community. To the rabbis in our community, our beautiful words were vulgar and profane. That week, our school ended our participation in the slam league.

But I couldn't accept that thousand-year-old ideas should dictate my own values and the meaning of my Jewishness. So that night, I rebelled in the only way I could. I watched hours of online slam poetry, violating the Sabbath for the first time in my life. That's when I started to spend my school's daily prayer time huddled in a bathroom stall, reading writings by the excommunicated Jewish scholar Baruch/Benedict Spinoza, and listening to my jazz favorites, Red Garland and Bill Evans.

Since then, I've found my own rhythm. I've done my best to foster diversity and acceptance within my Jewish community. I've worked with rabbis to create a Jewish philosophy-reading option at my school, as an alternative to praying with traditional liturgy. When I was elected to be the president of Bnei Akiva (our community's Jewish youth group), influential parents in the community demanded that I be replaced because I was not Orthodox. But I convinced the professional leadership of the program that there is value in exposing children to different points of view. In the end, I stayed.

Today, when the rest of my family leaves for Sabbath services, I stay home and play the piano, even though it's forbidden on the Sabbath. As I start the solo to "Have You Met Miss Jones" the notes speak about my love for slam poetry, and my pain when it was taken away. They sing about my illicit poetry-watching and my heretical reading during prayer. But just because I'm not at synagogue doesn't mean that I can't pray in my own way. It turns out that my mother was right; life isn't black and white. For me, these are the right notes. They're mine. And my Judaism is exactly that; it's my own.

REVIEW

Razi's essay synthesizes many personal achievements into an engaging narrative about defining his own Jewish identity and overcoming adversity within a traditional Orthodox community. He begins by discovering his passion for jazz, and its creative freedom, after years of playing classical piano. This scene simultaneously frames the essay's body and reveals another side of him. In the next section, he talks about being a Jewish slam poet, scholar, and youth leader. While Razi is not shy about his many accomplishments, he shares them tastefully by layering each personal fact into his stories. When his community's conservative Rabbis deemed his slam poetry too profane, ending his school's participation in the league, Razi was forced to reflect on his values and read more into Jewish philosophy.

Ultimately, Razi helped create a new prayer option for his school, and became president of the local Jewish youth group. This provides a sense of Razi's maturity and critical capacity. He concludes in the present, as he breaks Sabbath to play jazz piano at home. Linking the two proceeding sections is an excellent way to conclude. Although Razi's essay is chock-full of events, he ultimately avoids sounding clunky and remains engaging as each detail folds into a compelling central narrative.

—Dan Wood

TIANA MENON

Hometown: Grand Junction, Colorado, USA
High School: Public school, 260 students in graduating class
Ethnicity: Asian
Gender: Female
GPA: 4.5 out of 4.0
SAT: n/a
ACT: 33
SAT Subject Tests Taken: Mathematics Level 1, Literature
Extracurriculars: United States National Debate Team (Member of Olympic HS Debate Team), president of high school Speech and Debate Team, president of National Honor Society, intern with Senator Michael Bennet (DC Office), president of Girls Learn International
Awards: Valedictorian, National Champion in World Schools Speaking, State Champion of International Extemp
Major: Social Studies

ESSAY

"Overzealous—O-V-E-R-'ZED'-E-A-L-O-U-S—overzealous." I beamed while leaping off stage, proud of overcoming my two largest hurdles—public speaking and spelling. I apprehensively anticipated applause to fill the faux "class-itorium," but instead, my peers filled it with laughter and "You 'zed' it wrong's." Tears welled up in my eyes, but I knew this would happen. It always did. Whenever I pronounced words "The Indian Way," I was mercilessly teased for it; friends called it my

"Indian Problem." However, as I learned, it wasn't an "Indian Problem," there never was an "Indian Problem," but rather, a "Tiana Problem." My insecurities, fueled by my peers, overtook my sense of individuality—regardless of background, I wanted to blend in, not stand out.

Welcome to Grand Junction, Colorado—(Indian) Population: my family. My relationship with the "Valley" developed through paradox—it was a curse disguised as a blessing, a blessing disguised as a curse. I held the power to define the Indian stereotype, yet I felt powerless. This feeling was contagious; it slowly crept into my day-to-day routine. I began to detest what others loved, especially PE—and no, not because of the Asian stereotypes. Every day, the 6th period bell morphed the locker rooms into the ultimate hunting ground: *mean girls* would surround me, as a lion would its prey, roaring, "Evolution is real because Indians are as hairy as apes!" I spent the remainder of PE frantically trying to cover my arms and legs, my insecurities oozing (literally) from my pores. It wasn't my fault; I couldn't change who I was. Yet these girls preyed on the insecurities of a girl whose timid qualities rivaled a mouse—this was the curse.

"An Obama rally? In Grand Junction?" I questioned my parents, dumbfounded.

In response, my parents handed me a flyer emblazoned with his iconic "O." Several Facebook statuses later, Senator Obama strolled across the stage. As he told his story, I found myself relating to it. I'd always felt invisible because of arbitrary judgments that defined me, yet, his words gave me hope. I wanted to be like him—he, guided by overzealous rhetoric, commanded his audience's attention. Inspired by his confidence, I knew if I wanted to break my cycle of silence I had to learn how to speak publicly. Entranced, I ventured into the sea of blue-clad supporters. I felt lost in colorful waves; yet, I felt like I had discovered myself for the first time. I, too, needed speak up for myself: I refused to continue accepting my invisibility, my silence, my marginalization in the hope of change.

In the months following the rally, cartoons morphed into CNN; pumpkin patches into *Politico*; nights-out into newspapers. Politics became my world, and my world became empowered. Like the world of politics, I knew I didn't have to change myself, but rather, my 'voters' perspective. I wanted—I needed to be heard. I could be strong without being silent. Driven by my overzealous love of politics, I spoke out more during our class political discussions, presentations, and conversations. The more I spoke out, the less I held in—my newly outspoken persona surprised my tormentors. My stoic opposition to their teasing prompted them to stop. I was no longer "Tiana—unibrow-girl," but rather "Tiana—politics-girl." I redefined what an "Indian" meant to them. Being Indian didn't mean I was passive, it meant I was passionate; it didn't mean I was shy, but strong. Labels didn't define me; I defined them.

Now, six years later, I've learned to be overzealous in everything I do—politics, debate, volunteering. My actions, not my assumed identity, dictate my labels, my story, my passions. I choose to speak up, and I am heard. From being chosen to represent the United States internationally in debate to standing up to bullies, I am heard. The girl once terrified of speaking up, is speaking out; finally comfortable in her own skin. And if anyone thinks otherwise, I'll be sure to spell it out.

REVIEW

What is most striking about Tiana's essay is its manner of storytelling. Her writing immediately captures attention—she employs an engaging story as an introduction and her dialogue lede is striking—and manages to keep the reader's interest by pulling in thoughtful examples and utilizing a distinct tone. Tiana's voice pervades the entire essay making its story both personal and intimate; the reader easily feels understanding for her situation and sympathizes with the dilemma that she describes.

While Tiana's story touches on many points in her life (the spelling bee, bullying, an Obama rally, her increasing love of politics), Tiana is successful in presenting her personal growth succinctly: The reader can track her complete transformation from a girl defined by others' misconceptions to a girl able to create her own labels for herself. She does not spend time in extraneous details; every example she gives has a purpose. And her language, while noteworthy, is not excessive. Even the structure—one that follows each stage of her growth—is well planned and executed. Tiana's response to adversity is incredible in and of itself and successfully presents her attributes of vocalness and tenacity, but in the end, it is the way that she presents her struggles that makes her essay a notable and unforgettable read.

—Ha Le

Harriet Tieh

Hometown: Houston, Texas, USA
High School: Private school, 145 students in graduating class
Ethnicity: Asian
Gender: Female
GPA: 11.9 out of 11 (weighted)
SAT: Reading 800, Math 800, Writing 800
ACT: n/a
SAT Subject Tests Taken: Mathematics Level 2, Biology E/M, U.S. History
Extracurriculars: Varsity swim team, peer mentor, French club, Chinese club, Habitat for Humanity
Awards: French Honor Society, Cum Laude Society (PBK), AP Scholar with Honors
Major: Neurobiology

ESSAY

What is love? A promise at the altar? The soft kiss of water on parched lips? A flash of his shadowed gray eyes, or the tender caress of pink pigment on her cheekbones?

"I *love* those Jimmy Choos!"
       "I just love the pasta salad at *La Madeleine*."
  "Love you!"
      "Love ya more!"

Love. For a word describing such a powerful emotion, it is *always* in the air. The word "love" has become so pervasive in everyday conversation that it hardly retains its roots in blazing passion and deep adoration. In fact, the word is thrown about so much that it becomes difficult to believe society isn't just one huge, smitten party, with everyone holding hands and singing "Kumbaya." In films, it's the teenage boy's grudging response to a doting mother. At school, it's a habitual farewell between friends. But in my Chinese home, it's never uttered.

Watching my grandmother lie unconscious on the hospital bed, waiting for her body to shut down, was excruciatingly painful. Her final quavering breaths formed a discordant rhythm with the steady beep of hospital equipment and the unsympathetic, tapping hands of the clock. That evening, I whispered—into unhearing ears—the first, and only, "I love you" I ever said to her, my rankling guilt haunting me relentlessly for weeks after her passing. My warm confession seemed anticlimactic, met with only the coldness of my surroundings— the blank room, impassive doctors, and empty silence. I struggled to understand why the "love" that so easily rolled off my tongue when bantering with friends dissipated from my vocabulary when I spoke to my family. Do Chinese people simply love *less* than Americans do?

As I look back on seventeen years growing up in my Chinese family, I don't feel a gaping hole where "love" should be. I see my grandmother with her fluff of white hair, guiding my clumsy fingers as they grip the Chinese calligraphy brush, carefully dip *just enough* ink onto its thick bristles, and slowly smooth the pigment over tan parchment to form wobbly Chinese characters. I taste the sweet watermelon brought to my room at 3a.m. during finals week by a worried mother, and I hear the booming voice of my father begging me to get more sleep. I envision *baba*, dad, waiting in the 100°F heat every day to pick me up from school, just to drive home on traffic-infested roads. My *mama*, mother, staying home from work to care for my cold,

Cultural Identity

then feeling no resentment when she contracted it herself. My mistakes yielded stern, harsh lectures brimming with concern, while my tears assuaged *mama*'s irritation. I picture that arcane emotion imprinted in tacit smiles and hidden tears—shining from chests swollen with unabashed pride. Within the realm of my memories, I discovered a truth that lessened my crushing regret at the loss of my grandmother: just because the Chinese love, *ai*, can never render a fondness for Britney Spears' *Toxic* or be prostituted to mold descriptions of delicious dishes, the emotion isn't any more absent, or any less profound. Knowing that I could possibly have shared with my grandmother an implicit love that neither of us chose to address vocally, I could loosen my selfish grip on her past and allow her to ascend into her future.

Although the alien expression "wo ai ni, *mama, baba*," would be met with a few awkward blinks and a "How much money do you need?" expression, I feel the fondness for my joking father like "[g]reat drums throbbing through the air[,]" and for my stern mother in "great pulsing tides[,]," as Countee Cullen articulates in *Heritage*. We Chinese aren't *limited* by the cultural and linguistic "love" barrier; we learn, through living together as a family, through our shared experiences, the sensation of true devotion and compassion, and, if that's not something Americans call *love*, then I don't know what "love" is.

REVIEW

Harriet's nuanced take on the word "love" proves an effective window into her Chinese culture. Here, it turns from musings about love that leave the reader eagerly anticipating Harriet's connection to the topic to a personal account of family and identity. Throughout the essay, she maintains an emotional authenticity that doesn't feel sappy, which can be a delicate line to tread. A core strength of the essay is the way it demonstrates personal growth. It shows Harriet starting at a place of guilt for only professing her love to her grandmother once, and ends with her coming to terms with the ways that love is expressed differently in her family. Through the intimate details that Harriet provides about her childhood—such as her mother caring for her when she was sick—the reader gets a genuine sense of who she is and where she comes from.

While the essay overall reads smoothly, it could benefit from the simplification of some phrases and sentences. Clarity is more important than ornate language. Finally, the quote in the last paragraph feels unnecessary. In such an eloquent and personal essay, turning to someone else's words seems out of place. Despite these minor weaknesses, Harriet does an excellent job of writing an essay that demonstrates her insight, personal growth, and unique voice.

—Mia Karr

TYNAN JACKSON

Hometown: Plainfield, Illinois, USA
High School: Public school, 650 students in graduating class
Ethnicity: Biracial
Gender: Male
GPA: 5.67 out of 5.0
SAT: n/a
ACT: 33
SAT Subject Tests Taken: n/a
Extracurriculars: Spanish National Honor Society president, concert band first chair alto and District IMEA, jazz band lead alto, marching band drum major, math club (State freshman, sophomore, and senior year), intern for State Representative
Awards: National AP Scholar
Major: History and Literature

ESSAY

I am African-American, Caucasian, Jewish, and gay, and narrowly escaping the degradation of my ancestors: my great-great-great grandfather's slavery, my grandmother's persecution in the Holocaust, and the denial of gay identity. I am the personification of the culture and struggles of each of these groups. As I walk through life with this mix, I must be able to respect and love all different walks of life. Furthermore, during those times that I stereotype people, I assume roles onto their identity. I am able to stop myself and realize that they hold the wisdom from experiences that I do not, and that I am actually hurting myself. Judging a book by its cover really does make you miss out. Some people I know acknowledge me as the gay guy, a member of that small minority that is stricken with bullying and identity crisis, seldom as a Jew, or black. It has always been important to me for people to recognize me by my radiant personality and not by my superficial sexuality or race. My ethnicity and orientation do not define me: they are the tools my ancestors have granted so that I can pursue my destiny, and I have my individual spirit to color my path. I am an independent, positive person. I carry the mark of maturity with the essence of vitality. I can only hope that people remember me via my relationships with them and my effects on their lives. And so I apply the same mindset to others. The snappy, aggravated cashier at the grocery store checking me out may be working through her retirement to pay for her granddaughter's tuition. Or the black youth with his jeans hanging low and "speaking Ebonics" is actually executing a facet of his culture from which he takes pride and grows. Moreover my template also allows me to be open-minded; how could I not be cultural? My ancestors would not have succeeded without those that have listened and empathized with their plights. And how could I shut my ears? I cannot; I will not. I will not allow myself to shut out another's opinion simply because I was not introduced to their beliefs in my upbringing. How ignorant and arrogant to speak my gospel and thrive on the grace of others but not even consider others' words? Every breath I take is due to the grace of those magnanimous humans before me who not only listened to those Jews, or those slaves, or that gay person, but also took it upon themselves to advance humanity beyond close-mindedness into a world where every individual's contribution based on their experience is respected. There is never a time to neglect the social fragility of our existence, not in the courtroom or the living room. To assume the serenity of social culture is a blind eye to the macrocosm of daily life. It is my expectation to persevere for the fight for human rights and to respect the nature of all cultures and all peoples through my actions as well as my words. It is insufficient to tell someone they are wrong for persecuting. We have to help them find no solace in their prejudice. Not only do I have a duty to argue for the progress of our humanity, I will do so by example.

REVIEW

In this essay, Tynan immediately captures the reader's attention with a blunt confession of his complex identity before delving more deeply into how his identity has shaped his outlook on life.

This essay emphasizes the importance of struggles and challenges the narrowness of identity. Perhaps the most poignant strength of Tynan's piece is its message: that superficial aspects of identity do not define a person; rather, one's identity affects how one pursues his or her destiny. One aspect that I believe could have improved this essay is to break the thoughts into more than one paragraph as to give the reader a chance to breathe and pace him or herself. Despite this, Tynan's thoughts flow gracefully and logically throughout his writing, and the content pulled me in so I barely noticed that his essay functioned as one large paragraph.

Tynan shows his insightfulness and maturity both by acknowledging the strife his ancestors went through, but also by taking his acknowledgment and great respect for them and applying them to his own life. His writing is wise, powerful, and greatly moving, and the depth of his wisdom and maturity clearly impressed those who read it.

—Allison Yan

RAYLIN XU

Hometown: Glen Mills, Pennsylvania, USA
High School: Private school, 120 students in graduating class
Ethnicity: Asian
Gender: Female
GPA: 3.91 out of 4.0
SAT: Reading 800, Math 780, Writing 800
ACT: n/a
SAT Subject Tests Taken: Mathematics Level 2, Biology M, Chemistry, Spanish
Extracurriculars: Varsity tennis captain, varsity swimming captain, Mock Trial captain, Student Council Officer, A.I. duPont Hospital Volunteer
Awards: Diamond Challenge Grand Prize Winner, Lincoln Scholarship Essay, National Merit finalist, National Honor Society scholarship finalist, Pennsylvania Governors School for the Sciences Scholarship
Major: Human Developmental and Regenerative Biology

ESSAY

Clear, hopeful melodies break the silence of the night.

Playing a crudely fashioned bamboo pipe, in the midst of sullen inmates—this is how I envision my grandfather. Never giving up hope, he played every evening to replace images of bloodshed with memories of loved ones at home. While my grandfather described the horrors of his experience in a forced labor camp during the Cultural Revolution,

I could only grasp at fragments to comprehend the story of his struggle.

I floundered in this gulf of cultural disparity.

As a child, visiting China each summer was a time of happiness, but it was also a time of frustration and alienation. Running up to my grandpa, I racked my brain to recall phrases supposedly ingrained from Saturday morning Chinese classes. Other than my initial greeting of "Ni hao, ye ye!" ("Hello, grandpa"), however, I struggled to form coherent sentences. Unsatisfied, I would scamper away to find his battered bamboo flute, and this time, with my eyes, silently beg him to play.

Although I struggled to communicate clearly through Chinese, in these moments, no words were necessary. I cherished this connection—a relationship built upon flowing melodies rather than broken phrases. After each impromptu concert, he carefully guided my fingers along the smooth, worn body of the flute, clapping after I successfully played my first tentative note. At the time, however, I was unaware that through sharing music, we created a language of emotion, a language that spanned the gulf of cultural differences. Through these lessons, I discovered an inherent inclination toward music and a drive to understand this universal language of expression.

Years later, staring at sheets of music in front of me at the end of a long rehearsal, I saw a jumbled mess of black dots. After playing through "An American Elegy" several times, unable to infuse emotion into its reverent melodies that celebrated the lives lost at Columbine, we—the All-State Band—were stopped yet again by our conductor Dr. Nicholson. He directed us to focus solely on the climax of the piece, the Columbine *Alma Mater*. He urged us to think of home, to think of hope, to think of what it meant to be American, and to fill the measures with these memories. When we played the song again, this time imbued with recollections of times when hope was necessary, "An American Elegy" became more than notes on a page; it evolved into a tapestry woven from the threads of our life stories.

The night of the concert, in the lyrical harmonies of the climax, I envisioned my grandfather, exhausted after a long day of labor, instilling hope in the hearts of others through his bamboo flute. He played his own "elegy" to celebrate the lives of those who had passed. At home that night, no words were necessary when I played the alma mater for my grandfather through video call. As I saw him wiping tears, I smiled in relief as I realized through music I could finally express the previously inexpressible. Reminded of warm summer nights, the roles now reversed, I understood the lingual barrier as a blessing in disguise, allowing us to discover our own language.

Music became a bridge, spanning the gulf between my grandfather and me, and it taught me that communication could extend beyond spoken language. Through our relationship, I learned that to understand someone is not only to hear the words that they say, but also to empathize and feel as they do. With this realization, I search for methods of communication not only through spoken interaction, but also through shared experiences, whether they might involve the creation of music, the heat of competition, or simply laughter and joy, to cultivate stronger, more fulfilling relationships. Through this approach, I strive to become a more empathetic friend, student, and granddaughter as finding a common language has become, for me, a challenge—an invitation—to discover deeper connections.

REVIEW

In her essay, Raylin chooses the mundane over the grandiose—musical interactions with a family member over moments in an international chamber orchestra, for instance—to prove her point that the "cultural disparities" and "gulf" of comprehension that previously prevented her from reaching a harmony of understanding with her grandfather eventually dissolved once she realized that there are other, more personal ways to connect with people than language.

There's something intriguing about how Raylin orients the reader with as bright of an image as "clear, hopeful melodies," and then pairs it with something as somber as the image of a grandfather detained in a forced labor camp. That's a very poignant pairing, and it hooks the reader. For an admissions officer who sifts through countless essays about the all-important "I," a story that places the onus of the introduction on an entirely different individual is a welcome change from the usual.

This author showcases a very distinct claim over language. In some places, the poetic language serves to reinforce the topic of the essay: that language is not necessarily the sole way to connect with people. In some parts, though, the florid language encumbers the sentences and makes them somewhat awkward. In an essay that purports to recognize how incomplete language can be in conveying ideas, using clunky language seems like a betrayal of sorts to the reader. It's important to straddle eloquence and efficiency.

The epiphany conveyed in her final paragraphs is a truly mature one, and perhaps is what adds the final "oomph" to this essay. To see a high school student wring understanding from their everyday exploits proves they are capable of deep introspection—a trait that colleges crave in their student bodies.

—Brandon J. Dixon